For my teachers. Thank you.

CONTENTS

Contents ii

Foreward 1

A JAPANESE EXCHANGE 2

LUGGAGE TO LOFT 14

A TASTE OF TRUTH 26

LEAVING THIS BOX 30

AN HONEST DRAW 49

A LESSON IN HUMILITY 54

THE RELIGIOUS EXPERIENCE OF THE UFC 72

The UNINVITED VISITOR 90

FIGHTERS, PHILOSOPHERS, AND ATHLETES 96

THE ENGLISH PATIENT 110

INSTRUCTORS, BROTHERS, AND BLACKBELTS .. 116

KI, CHRIS, AND KUNDALINI 135

SOMEONE WATCHING OVER 153

THE JOURNEY CONTINUES 159

About the Author 161

FOREWARD

by Glenn Morris, Author of Path Notes of an American Ninja Master

As I said in Path Notes, not many Americans would elect to become "dojo boys" or in Japanese uchideshi. Roy Dean has proved me wrong on the American side, if not the numbers of this numerical theorem.

Mr. Dean describes the life of an American uchideshi and brings a unique viewpoint as well. He trained in Japan and typical of most adolescents (and many more adults) missed a lot of the experience but still managed to find a Judo hall that would accept him.

His is the voice of Generation X talking about his experiences of the tradition of budo. It is a real voice and informative to us "old silverbacks" who try to figure out why people get excited about the UFC. He discusses the choices some of us made so long ago we can't remember when they happened, but his fresh, raw perspective brings it back to the universal.

It is a good read.

A JAPANESE EXCHANGE

It's hard to remember a year in its entirety.

It's been said that people massively overestimate the changes they can accomplish in one year, while underestimating the changes they can make in five. While I agree that people can over-aspire, a year can definitely be life altering.

In that time, I went from working at a government job, driving a car, and having plenty of freedom, to living in a loft, commuting on foot, and getting thrown around by master martial artists.

I wish I could have written this book while the journey was happening, but the demands in the life of a martial apprentice did not allow me to even keep a brief journal.

So now, after the fact, I will piece together the account of a young man entering an adult world, in search of experience at a time in his life when the hunger for knowledge is insatiable. It's also the story of brothers coming together, and spirits connecting over time and distance.

Uchideshi is the Japanese term for a live-in student (literally: inside student). It is an apprenticeship to the master, and according to some traditions, the only way to access the finest details, hidden techniques, and inner workings of an art.

Some teachers consider the intensive, daily training of an uchideshi necessary to receive a teaching certificate, because only when you live in the dojo are you able to see the full spectrum of an art. How it's taught, how the students respond, the testing, the injuries, the challenges, and the endless stream of variables that life provides are best assimilated through the exposure that required training brings.

Often, the apprenticing student would be expected to carry out domestic responsibilities for the master: cleaning, preparing the meals and bath, massaging, and even taking care of the books. This is a very traditional arrangement, and I think you'd be hard pressed to find students willing to undergo that method in the modern world.

I'd wanted to be an uchideshi ever since I was a teenager. Why? I don't know. Even as a child, I had a fascination with Japan. I'd look at Japanese toy catalogs, admiring the warrior robots, wishing I understood the kanji. I loved the simplicity of Eastern architecture and design, expressing to my parents how I needed to simplify my room and put up screens as room dividers. At the international gift store, I'd pore over their selection of martial arts books, imagining the powers of their deadly practitioners.

For some reason I thought it was all really cool. Was this some kind of past life connection? Who knows, but I can see how it all added up to the next step.

I was fifteen, entering my sophomore year in high school, when I walked into my parent's bedroom and told them, "I need to get out of here." I felt an urge to leave Alaska and see the world. My mother suggested I speak to a school counselor about an exchange program.

I went the next day.

"Oh, you must have seen the signs!" my counselor exclaimed. Apparently flyers had been posted for weeks advertising Rotary Exchange programs. Though it was past the sign-up deadline, and interview times had already been assigned, she made a call for me.

The timing was perfect. Her connection at the Rotary Club had just hung up with a student who couldn't make it, so I slid into their spot. Days later I was at the interview doing my best to charm them, and left pleased with my performance.

But I made a mistake. A critical error. As I filled out the paperwork requesting the country I'd like to live in, there was the option of putting down a second and third country.

Being a brash young man, I made an assumption that everything would go my way, and put only one selection as my country of choice: Sweden.

For choices two and three, I smugly wrote, "Any other country in the world." Five months later, I received a phone call congratulating me on being selected to go to Japan. I tried to change it back to Sweden, but it was too late.

It was meant to be, whether I liked it or not.

So I went. To be honest, it was a difficult time. Many books and movies have been made on Westerners clashing with Eastern customs. It was all of that and more.

It was not easy removing myself from friends and family, and being transplanted to a place where you can't speak the language, or even read the alphabet. It was sensory overload, and I had no one to blame for this situation but myself.

Japan is definitely different. It's not a petite island version of America with an exotic language. It is more paradoxical than you can believe. The insects were huge, but everything else was compact and narrow.

The area where I lived (Toyokawa, Aichi Prefecture) was hot and humid in the summer. This cannot be overstated. Winter was brisk, with a touch of snow now and then, and embraced without central heating at home or school. Too hot or too cold, it was never just right, and the only constant was year-round discomfort.

The Japanese believe it's important for the young to learn how to gaman, or bear discomfort well. I agree that's important to toughen up each new generation, but at the time, I wasn't that receptive to doing things that were good for me.

I wanted to party with my friends. I wanted to hang out with Swedish blondes. I was a self-absorbed glutton of everything around me. I was an American teenager.

The life of a Japanese teenager is different than our own. High school in Japan is a lot like college in the USA. It's highly competitive, and everyone wants to get into the oldest and most established high schools to increase their chances of getting into a good university.

Newer high schools had difficulty attracting top students, so if they wanted to attract the best and the brightest, they needed a hook. Internationalism was very fashionable, so my school used exchange students (i.e. me), as a public relations vehicle to lure in talented kids. I felt antagonistic toward them in using me for PR, and even more so because they denied it, but I did my duty and played along. Gaman.

In other respects, my high school functioned like a military academy. There was a French military uniform to go along with the regulation book bag, which was strapped to your regulation bike. Hair and nail inspections were practiced, and makeup and piercings not allowed. Even in the wintertime, no additional clothing was allowed. My school was reputed to be one of the strictest in Japan, and they were bent on proving it.

It was standard practice for those who had committed an infraction to line up in a hallway, backs against the wall, and wait for a teacher or administrator. Teachers would warm up by yelling, gradually working their way to a frenzy, which included throwing books down the hallway, and occasionally punching or kicking a wall. And it worked. Students broke into tears. For more severe transgressions, the hair had to go. Boys had their heads shaved, while girls simply had it bobbed off.

While other Rotary exchange students were partying on the beaches of Rio de Janeiro, exploring the wonders of Africa, or frolicking with Swedish beauties, I was stuck in the West Point of the Orient. Even though my classmates were friendly, and my host families were patient and accepting, I felt like I had been globally shafted.

Undoubtedly, one thing that got me through that difficult year was discovering the art and sport of judo. There was a policy for international students to actively study a traditional Japanese art after school. Kyudo (archery), kendo (sword fighting), sado (tea ceremony), and ikebana (flower arranging) were among the options presented, but I chose judo. My advisor warned me that judo training was very severe, but that was fine by me. I was in a state of mind that welcomed the challenge.

Linguistically, I should have been more prepared for the year. I didn't know any Japanese when I went, so I couldn't just sit in a classroom and understand what was happening.

Instead, I spent a lot of time in the library with other exchange students. Together, we studied Japanese and I joined my assigned class for physical education, music, and English. At the end of the year, I could have asked for a diploma stating a year of full credits, but I chose not to and returned to Alaska a year behind my friends, as an academic junior.

I investigated early graduation, but my counselor couldn't work it out with the "lost year." I deeply regretted not asking for academic credits while in

Japan, but at that point it was too late. I considered dropping out of school, and just taking the GED exam, but figured that could end up haunting me later.

My teachers, concerned for me, urged me to do something different for my senior year. It could be as simple as going to a different school, leaving the state, or taking off on an adventure. I didn't know what I was going to do, and I was pretty depressed. Something had to be done.

Then an opportunity arose. I was able to move to Canada and live with a relative in North Bay, Ontario, a resort town about three hours northeast of Toronto. He had room in his house, I would take Grade 13 classes where the students were my age, and it would be a totally new scene.

All that was true, but the one drawback was a lack of martial arts training. No judo, just karate and kickboxing. I studied karate with one of my friends, but spent the majority of my time reading and dreaming about aikido. I convinced myself that this was the ultimate art to learn. It was a sophisticated form of jujutsu that smoothly redirected an attacker's energy against them. Fighting without fighting. It all made so much sense.

I bought every book regarding aikido, learning everything I could about the art and its founder, Morihei Ueshiba. Ultimately, I bought it all: the theory, the philosophy, and the legends. But I couldn't train. Nothing was available in the area, so I seethed and bided my time until I went back to Alaska. I would learn this invincible art of peace in my frozen homeland.

Returning to Anchorage, I immediately signed up at the local dojo, Aikido North, and began training with all my might. I was attending the University of Alaska so I could keep my job with the government as a "stay-in-school" student, but my job there was really just to support my martial arts training.

I trained diligently for two years, falling in love with the circularity of aikido, the aesthetic beauty of the movements, and the efficiency of blending with a committed attack. The people at the dojo were wonderful, and I looked forward to the daily practices.

It was through one of the instructors there that I came into jujutsu and the connection to becoming an uchideshi was made. Ken Blaylock taught aikido on Mondays, and one night after class, he related his experiences during a recent trip to Japan.

He accompanied his jujutsu teacher, Julio Toribio, as they studied under ninjitsu Grandmaster Maasaki Hatsumi and Machida Kenshinsai, a Japanese sword instructor. I could relate to what Ken was saying through my own experiences in Japan, and was wowed by his confirmation of some mystical and energetic aspects of martial arts I had only read about.

When Ken began teaching Julio Toribio's jujutsu style, Seibukan, I quickly enrolled as a student, hoping to learn the roots of aikido. He taught on Sundays, and while other aikido students would occasionally drop in to play in class, I became his only regular student. He put a lot of energy into me, and over time I inquired whether I could be an uchideshi for Sensei Toribio (hereafter referred to simply as Sensei).

I investigated several live in student programs for aikido students, but never found anything that felt like it would've been the right fit. This included the consideration of going back to Japan to study, but I decided against it for several reasons. Not only would it have been prohibitively expensive, but I knew far too well the additional pains a foreigner had to endure while training in Japan. I wanted the opportunity to invest my efforts in the training itself, without wasting time overcoming cultural and linguistic barriers.

Ken spoke to Sensei, and on his recommendation, I was accepted into the program. Both suggested that I travel to Monterey, see the dojo, and check everything out, just as you'd visit a university before enrollment. That would have been ideal, but I couldn't afford it. I didn't have the money to fly down, so I simply trusted that everything would work out. In fact, I steeled myself to do whatever it took to make it work out.

I had a lot of expectations that this experience would take me to a new level of martial artistry that I had, so far, been unable to achieve. But beyond physical progress, I felt that the intensity and volume of training I had to endure to complete a full year would somehow legitimize me. As a man. As a rite of passage.

I wasn't sure what it was I had to prove, but if I could do this, I felt that something inside of me could rest. Something inside of me had to have this adventure. Until I had completed the journey, there was no way I could go to college and focus on schoolwork, because I wasn't willing to sacrifice for something I wasn't truly passionate about. At that time, martial arts were my passion, not academic achievement.

Obviously, this is shortsighted, since education will serve an individual far better than physical prowess in the modern world, but I had to be honest with myself. This is what I loved.

So I took a chance, and hopped on a plane. I had lived away from home for two years in two different countries, but they were very controlled, prearranged situations. This was different.

I had written Sensei an introductory letter a few months before leaving Alaska, and had spoken to him on the phone a few weeks before I arrived, but it still wasn't a lot of communication. I rolled the dice and left for Monterey, hoping for the best, and resolute to live through the worst.

Amazingly, it all worked out. There were injuries and conflicts, relationships and reunions, trials and celebrations. Programs were established, precedence set, minds opened and secrets revealed. It was a year that exceeded every expectation, every preconceived notion I harbored, and in the end, satisfied the hunger that hadn't allowed me to focus on other areas of my life. In retrospect, it seems almost scripted, almost meant to be.

Near the end of my stay in the dojo, I called home to Alaska, asking my mother to send me the roll of Japanese certificates I had thrown in a drawer years before. I told her to send them all to me, even though there was only one I was interested in. I wanted to have my shodan (first degree black belt) certificate in judo framed, and I knew it might end up in the trash or lost in storage if someone got the urge to clean out that drawer.

I received the certificates a few weeks later and had a Japanese friend translate them, just out of curiosity, before I threw the others away. I took a little journey to the past as she read aloud the titles of certificates I received, including one for a ski trip and another for a speech contest for international students.

Then she came across one I wasn't expecting. "This one," she began,"is some sort of certificate from a Japanese school. It says that you completed the requirements for one year at Mito Koko. Is that the school that you went to?"

I couldn't believe it. There it was, the credits for the "lost year" that had held me back in high school. I looked at the certificate: It was written in English. It may have been presented to me while I was in Japan, or sent along with my shodan certificate after I had left the country. I have no idea how I got it, but it was here now, right in front of me.

If I had known that I received it, I would have never lived in Canada, resolved to master aikido, made the connection with Sensei, or become an uchideshi. I probably would have graduated with everyone else and gone off to college, suffered through, and gotten a job. The entire course of my life changed because I needed a piece of paper I already had in my possession.

If I had only known, I'd be living in a different world, without ever enduring the pain and injuries that serious training demands from its participants. In short, I never would have become the martial artist I am today.

I'm so glad I never found it.

LUGGAGE TO LOFT

If I wanted to be an uchideshi, I needed to earn some money. As much as I could in the shortest possible timeframe. I wasn't sure how much I needed, or how much Sensei was going to charge me over the course of the year, so I just played the denial game.

It seems funny to say it now, but I was so resolute on creating this kind of experience, I really didn't want to know how much it was going to cost in case it turned out to be more than I could afford. I was just going to save as much money as I could, and if it wasn't enough, I'd work something out. This adventure was happening, no matter what.

After graduating from high school in Canada and going back to Alaska, I worked as a "stay-in-school student" for the National Transportation Safety Board (NTSB). The field office I worked for investigated airplane accidents. Basically, I was a secretary, but it was a great job with all the perks of being with a sharp government agency: a pleasant working environment, intelligent co-workers, sick leave, and my own parking space. This lasted until someone in Washington deemed my position unnecessary and cut it's funding.

My supervisor at the NTSB allowed me to remain as long as I wanted that summer, paying my salary out of the agency's travel fund. I stayed on until August, then got a job carrying bags for a cruise line.

It was a terrible job, and one I was poorly suited for. It didn't take a lot of mental horsepower to grab bags off a conveyor belt and throw them into trucks and trains, but it did require a certain amount of common sense, which I lacked. I couldn't stop making mistakes in this gig, and anticipated dismissal at every turn.

I took the job because they needed people to work tons of overtime. At $6.25 an hour, I needed to put in a lot of effort to build my own travel fund.

I don't know if I was necessarily in the wrong place at the wrong time, but having that job was like gambling with borrowed money. I needed it so desperately to attain my goal of becoming a live in student that somehow, I lost touch with common sense and remained defensively employed. In other words, I just didn't want to get fired.

One of the few things that brightened my long days was a friendship I developed with a fellow crew member named Chris. We hit it off, and the shifts we spent together moved from mere tolerability to actual enjoyment. He was bright, and having already completed two years of college, was taking a year off before finishing up the last half.

I've always held that strong bonds in male relationships are forged through loyalty and time, so it's rare when two strangers fall easily into sync. Others noticed it as well. My manager chided me, "So, I hear you and Chris are buddy buddy there, eh?"

It was true, and it was fun sharing our separate interests with the other. He took me rock climbing, I introduced him to aikido and BJJ, and we celebrated his twenty-first birthday in style: Dining at one of the finest restaurants in town, followed by a long night of partying.

Moving forward to Monterey, I left it all behind: Family, friends, training partners, patterns and habits. My old life was fading as a new one began. I needed something different in my life, and I felt that this apprenticeship was it. I didn't know exactly what it would entail, but I'd figure that out shortly.

Arriving in Monterey, an Instructor from the dojo picked me up, took me out for some training, then deposited me back at my new home. As I checked out my living quarters, I thought, "Hmmm... not spacious." Then again, at least I had something. I'd sleep on the mat if I had to.

My living space was a loft, originally used for storage, recently cleared to accommodate two college kids from Kansas who did a three-month uchideshi stint. There was already a futon on industrial carpet in the 5-by-15 foot space, so I simply laid my sleeping bag on top of it and got the rest of my personal items arranged in my tiny new home.

As unglamorous as it seems, this was my dream, and the giddiness I experienced by living out my goals translated into an insatiable appetite for training. Believe me, training was plentiful, but I still couldn't get enough. Initially, that is.

My required training schedule was full. Monday's evening classes began with a 5:15, plus a 7:00. Tuesday had the kids' classes at 5:30 (which I was forced to participate in, despite strong protests), a 7:00, and a weapons class at 8. Wednesday repeated the 5:15 and 7:00 schedule, then added iaido at 8:30.

Thursday repeated Tuesday's schedule, with a black belt class replacing weapons at 8 p.m. On Friday evenings, Sensei taught ninjitsu, so that was a day of rest for me (for the first few months, at least). Classes resumed at 9 a.m. on Saturday. Sunday was also a day of rest, but I usually did some sort of training on my own, feeding my compulsion.

When you add it all up, 12 classes a week doesn't seem so bad, but a host of other factors were taking up my time, and breaking down my body. In becoming an uchideshi, you have, in effect, become a martial serf: Your body is no longer your own, it belongs to the dojo. If somebody dreams up a crazy technique and wants to try it out, the uchideshi is there and always willing to train. If higher-ranked students are offering instruction to newer ones and need an uke (training partner), you're it. If a pretest is occurring, 9 times out of 10 you're involved, getting thrown and absorbing techniques.

Additionally, once your ukemi (rolling and falling skills) is deemed suitable, Sensei will use you to demonstrate techniques, which keeps you on your toes and further cuts down your rest time.

Every time students train in Seibukan Jujutsu, they go through the same warm-up sequence, which includes a variety of hand strikes, kicks, and falling exercises. Even by the end of my term, I didn't mind participating in any of the classes (they were almost always fun), I was just tired of doing the same warm-ups, day in and day out. Since I had to do them, every day, for a long period of time, those skills and movements were ingrained into my body. I guess that's really the thrust behind required training, you're going to get better, whether you want to or not. I think about the thousands and thousands of rolls I took in classes over the year, and note a definite difference.

I always thought I had good ukemi to begin with. In Japan, the head judo coach of my school, Kakihara Sensei, wouldn't let me get on the mat with the other players before I learned some protective falling skills. I learned ukemi two hours a day, five days a week, for six weeks. After the first week, as angles were shaved and my body rounded out, two circular bruises appeared near my shoulder blades, each four to five inches in diameter.

Every time I rolled, it hurt. Every time I fell, it hurt. Every time I slapped, it hurt. I was miserable. I told them this. They responded by telling me that if I did it correctly, it wouldn't hurt. They were right, of course, but my body was at a point where everything produced pain. Finally, after six weeks, I took their ukemi test and passed. When I look back on it, I think my skills were acceptable weeks earlier, but they held off because my gi hadn't yet been received in the mail.

Although I cursed them at the time, I've thanked them years after for saving me on many occasions. There have been countless situations where my body has simply responded to a surprise throw or an unusual takedown, protecting me in the process. But even though my ukemi was satisfactory in protecting me from major damage, that doesn't mean there wasn't room for improvement.

Daily Seibukan practices refined my protective skills as a martial artist, which is one of the benefits I was hoping for. I longed for a day when the movements of a martial art would be so infused into my body that no thought would be necessary to initiate appropriate action. Direct entries to off-balance an opponent, getting off the line of attack and delivering a strike, spotting and directing my opponents into their balance points-all of these are concepts and movements repeated over and over again through kata (forms), tai sabaki (body movement), and other Seibukan exercises. Having to be there, class after class, day after day, removes the magic of the movements. After a while, what you may have thought of as a cool technique turns to merely something that you do. Then you move on and keep training.

On some level for me, being an uchideshi was an ego trip involving hours on the mat. I trained a lot in Alaska doing aikido, but it still was never enough. Training, in itself, is significant to me. I feel that the consistency and volume of training a student undergoes is a reflection of his character and dedication to an art. If you train a lot, in my book, you're a serious martial artist, even if you're not as quick to catch on to things as others are. Adopting the discipline of consistent training is what really shows your mettle over the long haul.

I was already diligent about going to class, but by forcing myself into a heavy regimen of required training, I was discovering who I was as an individual and as a martial artist. It was my own manhood ritual and rite of passage. I almost joined the military, looking for the same sort of masculine vindication, but decided on an uchideshi program instead. It's what I really wanted, and it's exactly what I got once I found the right place.

How much training can you take? That's the question my ego was asking, and my body was slowly formulating an answer. The first three months, armed with enthusiasm, I was easily able to take more training than the schedule required. By the time I hit six months, the toll of multiple daily practices started to wear on me, and the thrill had somehow waned. At the end of the year, training was nothing special at all; it's just what I did. I ended up staying another quarter, totaling 15 months, and by the end of my term, I had definitely had as much training as I could take. Actually, the last month I was there, my body fell apart.

It was a mental release with physical manifestations. I absorbed a lot of techniques, took gobs of ukemi, trained like a madman, but remained injury free for more than a year. Of course, there were little sprains and tears here and there, but overall, I just kept ticking because I knew I couldn't afford to get hurt. But that last month, I had already left the dojo mentally, so with my body still hanging out and participating, I paid a very real price for my lack of integration. My left wrist was trashed, right arm hyperextended, neck tweaked, hips misaligned, the list goes on and on. I was tired, too. Not tired of training, or tired of classes, but just tired of the lifestyle.

Since I didn't have a lot of money, eating out regularly wasn't an option. People knew my situation well (hey, they trained in my living room), so they sometimes brought me leftovers, and occasionally invited me into their homes for dinner.

My caloric intake was just too low for the daily energy expenditure training required, and consequently, I dropped well over 10 pounds. Unfortunately, none of it was fat. After 15 months, people told me I looked pretty gaunt and haggard, which is not always the most pleasant thing to hear, but it was the truth, and they mentioned it only out of concern.

I also longed for a shower. We didn't have one in the dojo, nor hot water, so I'd walk a couple blocks to the Coast Guard Marina and use the quarter-operated shower stall for divers. Not a huge deal.

What was a huge deal was getting sick. If I was legitimately sick or injured, there was no expectation for me to train until I healed. So training wasn't the issue; a healing environment was. Without any heating, and oftentimes alone, having the flu or even a cold in an empty dojo can be miserable. It's hard to imagine you're recuperating quickly when you wake up and see your breath.

Despite the reduction in my standard of living, living in the dojo was magical. After the last people had left and lights flipped off, only I was there to break the silence with soft steps on the mat. The movements and exertions of the day were past, but something still dusted the air. It wasn't like entering a barren warehouse or abandoned building, where the sense of vacant space can overwhelm you. Even without anybody in it, the dojo was never empty; it was simply still, like some kind of martial cathedral. I'd put Jewel in the stereo, sit back, and listen as her voice reverberated off the cavernous angles. Or, if there were other uchideshi there, I'd put in U2 and we'd do a midnight training in the dark. Or maybe we'd dance. It didn't matter; the playground was ours to do what we wished.

Other uchideshi would come in periodically, some for a few days, others much longer. Although I liked having the place to myself, it was great having company, and some very strong friendships were formed since intense experiences bond people closely. The only thing about having extra uchideshi in the house was the fact that most were on vacation. They wanted to live it up, stay up late, and make the most of being away from home. Those of us who were in it for the long haul, however, couldn't afford to talk all night or eat out, especially when Sensei would lead special morning classes for the visitors. Their vacation was our daily life, so our ability to burn the candle at both ends was brief at best.

My day-to-day routine was pretty regimented. I'd wake up at about eight in the morning and prepare the dojo: vacuuming, straightening up and organizing the public areas before Sensei came in and began teaching private lessons. I'd cram down some breakfast and head off to work at nine, returning home a little after four o'clock, which gave me a small window of decompression before I was on the mat at 5:15 to begin training.

A couple times over the year, I lay there in the loft and wondered if I could keep it all together. There was so much energy going out into work and training that I had to really be efficient in taking care of the day-to-day stuff. I went shopping on my lunch breaks and changed loads between classes at the laundromat across the street. I made friends with the homeless guys so they'd look out for my clothes and made sure no one stole them. There was at least one occasion where the Wasted Knights of Cannery Row stood in defense of my clothing.

It was an exceptionally productive time, and over the course of the year, I feel that I really learned what jujutsu was all about. From a physical standpoint, it's using distraction, angles, leverage, and proper coordination of body weight to create the largest effect with the least amount of effort.

Beyond that, it's making the most of the time that's available to you, and creating results that may seem spectacular to the uninitiated observer. Jujutsu is about fighting smart and living efficiently. There's no magic involved; it's just hard work and consistency magnified by guidance on where to direct your energy.

Because I lived it, it's difficult to have an objective, outside perspective of how being an uchideshi has changed me. It certainly settled something deep within that I had been longing for, and satisfied a thirst for martial knowledge at a special time when personal responsibilities in my life were minimal, allowing dedication to match desire.

In its entirety, the experience was fascinating. I was able to observe the difference between the Monday/Wednesday and the Tuesday/Thursday crowd at the dojo; participate in classes taught by all the teachers; note the effectiveness of their methods and stylistic distinctions; see the progression of physical prowess in students from their first day on; endure subjugation to runaway egos bolstered by rank; and much, much more.

From challengers, shysters, and mystical believers to the emotional ramifications of true self-expression, everyone I met, everything that happened, and everything taught, intentionally or not, became part of me. You never know how much you can learn until you're pushed or overwhelmed, and this kind of experience can certainly do that. It's not just about training in an art; it's about living it.

Every class, every day, is a little bit different in the way it's taught and perceived, according to each individual's level of skill. Attempts to verbally recreate the physical activity of training, nuances of growth, and daily class variations in a book would be pedantic. Instead, what I've chosen to focus on are the stories, insights, and experiences that occurred on this lightly trodden path, rather than on an overly technical description of the vehicle itself.

I've always believed being an uchideshi was an elite position, and I did my best to represent this ideal. There is an assumption and expectation that the volume and severity of training allows the technical requirements of the system to be passed cleanly, through direct transmission, from master to student.

Whether it's Sokaku Takeda teaching Morihei Ueshiba in exchange for serving him in his home, or Ken Shamrock taking fighters in to live at the Lion's Den, the pattern of young warriors hungry for knowledge and experience seeking guidance under masters is perpetual. Through this closeness in their respective classrooms, the transmission of wisdom may be so thorough and complete that students may eventually transcend their teacher's accomplishments.

If they're successful in doing so, it's a powerful testament to the depth of their instructor's knowledge and teaching ability. As years go by, teachers will continue to live through their students, in their movements, and those students will eventually pass the flame to the next generation. It's a timeless cycle.

As an uchideshi, you are also the physical embodiment of the dojo's spirit. If you're not on the mat, it's noted. Your only job is to train with a smile on your face. That's not difficult; after all, you're doing what you love, and doing a lot of it, at that. It was my dream to be an uchideshi, a modest one perhaps, but it certainly held significance for me.

I bet there are people just as hungry as I was, aching for an opportunity to fully invest themselves in an art. If you get the chance, take it. You will not be the person you thought you'd be at the end of it. You'll still be you, but after all the adventures that constitute an uchideshi experience, you'll be a different cat. I certainly am, but I know it was the best decision I've ever made.

A TASTE OF TRUTH

I received my first degree black belt in Judo in less than a year, in Japan, from the Kodokan. How is this possible?

I fought for it.

It's a beautiful thing. There was a written test for the rules, a kata requirement, and a point total amassed from tournament wins. The point total was, in fact, the real test for shodan. Actually, it was so challenging that I almost didn't receive it.

I was enthusiastic when I joined the judo club at my Japanese high school. After I had learned ukemi, and was finally allowed on the mat, I sparred with our team captain, Ichikawa, on the first day of practice. It was a total massacre. Every time I grabbed him, I wound up on the ground. Immediately, I got up and charged to repeat the process, while Ichikawa smiled. He liked the fact that I didn't give up, even though the situation was hopeless.

To me, he was throwing me easily, effortlessly, at will. He wasn't even breaking a sweat, and I was trying my best. The only thing I truly knew was, whatever he was doing, it was magical, and I wanted that same kind of power.

I now realize that I had a potent combination of factors going for me in studying judo, the kind of combination that can create success in almost any athletic endeavor.

I was motivated, hungry to eat pain, fairly strong, somewhat flexible, and most importantly, relatively fearless. At 16 years old, your body heals instantly, and nothing seems to get out of whack.

I trained hard the first five months, and tasted immediate success as I rolled through my opponents each month at the local shiai (competition). I was stronger than most of the Japanese players, and taller as well (which has its own advantages and disadvantages in this sport), so I started skipping practices and coasting on my natural abilities.

In order to move up in the promotional system, I obtained points by beating a required number of competitors who were equally ranked. At each rank, the number of opponents increases. It didn't dawn on me that while I was coasting, the competition I would now face was far more skilled than anything I'd seen in the past. Soon I would understand.

I showed up at the next competition without having practiced a whole lot, especially in the two weeks prior. I don't feel like delving too deeply into this, but let's just say that each time I stepped on the mat that day, I had my ass handed to me in a very thorough and complete manner.

One of the members of my Rotary club came to see me in action that day. Witnessing the dismal performance, he immediately took me under his wing. Mr. Natsumi had been an excellent judo player in his youth, only losing once in his competition career, and saw that I was in need of some tutelage.

I went home to my host family and they, of course, asked how it went. I told them that I didn't want to talk about it. I'm sure that my host father and Mr. Natsumi convened at the next Rotary meeting to discuss a remedy. Shortly thereafter, Mr. Natsumi was picking me up at the house after my club judo practice and taking me to the community dojo to train with more bodies. He encouraged me to bow to the most formidable master there, Igami Shoten, for sparring, who easily deflected my best attacks and casually threw me at will.

This man was a master and I had no chance. If I held both my hands flat, palms together, perhaps they would equal one of his hands. Still, he took a liking to me, and soon after, Mr. Natsumi was also taking me to Igami Shoten's home dojo for his classes, on top of the community dojo schedule, and daily school practices. After every training session, Mr. Natsumi would treat me to a cold soda or ice cream. Because of his kindness, things really started to click. Progress had begun once again.

That was the first time I realized how much better you could get when you trained constantly, every day, and planted the dream seed of becoming an uchideshi. Since I was training like a madman, I started winning again at the tournaments, and I eventually amassed enough points by the end of the year to receive my shodan.

It's elegant in its simplicity. You train; you fight. If you win, you advance. If you lose, you learn, and you're motivated to train harder and try again. Judo is a microcosm of life, and a timeless vehicle for development.

Judo gave me the gift of martial truth. One you taste it, it's never forgotten, and you can recognize where it exists, and where it no longer lives.

LEAVING THIS BOX

I remember my last judo competition very clearly. There weren't that many judo players in my weight class in Alaska, so they lumped us together in an open category. The first match I had was against a guy roughly my size, and I threw him quickly with an uchimata (inner-thigh throw).

My next match pitted me against this big brown belt, a middle-aged guy with a thick beard, weighing in around 215 pounds. When we squared off, he dragged me around the mat like a rag doll. I was about 165 at the time, so I was giving up some weight, but I should have been craftier in my approach and found a way to throw him.

But I didn't, I ended up losing the match, and as competitors know, there's nothing like a loss to leave a lasting impression. It really made me think, "Man, there's got to be a better way."

After all, if I had been on the street, I would have been dead. This guy was a monster, and my technique was not good enough to overcome that kind of size, strength, and weight disparity. Thus, the search began for a new art to add to what I already knew, an art that would be able to transcend size and strength through effortless technique. Over time, the research I had done pointed very clearly to the next art for me to study: aikido. But where do you think my initial exposure to aikido came from?

Steven Seagal. Years before I ever thought of training in martial arts, I watched "Above the Law," with my brother, listening very intently as he told me what it was this guy was doing that made him so deadly. Mr. Seagal, he patiently explained, practiced aikido, an art developed for close-quarter combat by monks. They lived in very small cubicles, and consequently, their movements were very tight and circular. I thought it was incredible that such a mysterious art could have evolved from the cramped solitude of warrior monks, but I bought it, since he knew something about which I knew nothing, by default alone, he obviously knew what he was talking about.

Although my initial exposure to aikido was through Steven Seagal, I realize it's not always fashionable to say so, particularly in aikido circles (I have heard, "What he does is not aikido" from more than one instructor). But let's be frank, he brought aikido into the spotlight, straight to the masses, and basically showed the world how aiki-techniques would be applied in the street. He's the real deal, just listen to his Japanese! Watching one of his movies is enough to entice an individual to investigate what appears to be a very effective martial art.

So I investigated. Solely through book research, I found myself "buying" into the art entirely: hook, line and sinker. I pored over <u>Aikido and the Dynamic Sphere</u>, I read and reread Koichi Tohei's <u>Ki in Everyday Life</u>, and bought every book I could get my hands on that mentioned aikido. Because I didn't have any access to instruction in the town of North Bay, my thought was by gathering all the information I could, I'd be ahead of the ball game when I actually began to train under a legitimate instructor. This was true. I thoroughly memorized the biography of Morihei Ueshiba (also known as O'Sensei), his incredible feats of mystical power, and the evolution of Daito-Ryu Aiki-Jujutsu into aikido. Unfortunately, all this reading without a physical reality check cast an aiki spell over me, leaving me unable to retain a sliver of objectivity or skepticism. Ultimately, I believed it all.

A particular passage in Tohei's book had a very profound effect in shaping my perspective. He recollected an early aikido demonstration in Hawaii, during which he was attacked, somewhat suddenly, by several highly ranked judo players. He threw them all, effortlessly, and noted with amusement how many spectators found it unbelievable that he could throw such large, skilled men with movements that looked like dancing! I was mesmerized by his account. I couldn't believe I had wasted all that time and effort in judo when an aikido practitioner could put down several judo players easily.

Other books only solidified the case that aikido was an invincible art. The story that clinched my devotion was Kenji Tomiki, the noted educator and judo exponent, recalling how even though he had fought almost every good judo and jujutsu man in the world at that time, he was decimated after challenging Morihei Ueshiba. O'Sensei even gave him another chance, and after finding himself mysteriously thrown to the other end of the mat, Tomiki bowed to Ueshiba and acknowledged that he'd like to become his student.

Testimonials from noted martial artists, the philosophy of nonaggression, the defensive nature of the techniques, the theoretical superiority of the turning movements, and the mystical powers of Morihei Ueshiba, all of these added up to a convincing argument that aikido was the best. The best art for me, the best martial art. I had finally found exactly what I thought a martial art should be, and what I'd been looking for.

Why would I want to study anything else when I'd be able to defeat somebody with his own strength and aggression? The daydream scenarios that stemmed from this idea were intoxicating. Imagine this:

A wild haymaker is thrown by an enraged man. Instead of crudely blocking and counter striking, I smoothly blend with his attack, throwing him to the ground. His spirit diminished, he continues to lie there, as the realization sinks in that his own aggression led to his defeat. I stand unscathed, and with a heart heavy for the human condition, walk away into the night (often with a girl in tow), as the crowd gathered outside of the bar stares in awed silence.

Although it would be impossible to prove, I'd be willing to wager that most aikido students secretly long for an opportunity to see if their stuff "really works." I've seen it written about, I've heard it quietly discussed. I'll freely admit that I was looking forward to the day when I'd turn the corner and have a man run at me, hand raised above his head, cueing me that a shomen (front) strike was on the way. Luckily, the philosophy of aikido keeps most people out of trouble, or at least from searching out and picking fights. But even the best philosophy cannot completely quash the ego, destroy the delusional expectations of the practitioners, or monitor the internal itch to elevate practice beyond repetitious physical exercises. That's when things get dangerous.

Aikido has beautiful, aesthetically pleasing techniques that are a lot of fun to do, practiced in an environment where resistance is discouraged. If a person has no experience in a martial art or athletic activity where resistance is applied, it's easy to confuse attacks that come at you in the dojo with a real attack on the street. Depending on the crowd you run with, an average person may have witnessed one or two real fights in their lives, past the levels of elementary and secondary school. Before the advent of the UFC, how many people had ever seen skilled martial artists or street fighters throw down and really fight?

In my experience, I've found that most aikido practitioners are white, middle-aged professionals who don't witness violence on a regular basis. It's not in their daily environment, in their neighborhood, or in their jobs. It's not something they would even consciously address or worry over. Why would it even enter their minds? You're not going to get mugged in the suburbs, tackled in front of the company water cooler, or jumped at your kid's soccer game. Which is good. Nobody wants to live in a risky environment or a bad neighborhood. However, when defenses for attacks aren't referenced with reality, techniques become more and more removed from combat effectiveness.

Combat effectiveness is one of the major reasons I study martial arts. Some people aren't, and are interested foremost in Japanese culture, cultivation of mystical powers, light physical exercise, or social interaction in a clean, healthy environment. That's great, but there should be some sort of caveat explaining that although the roots of aikido are rooted in war, combat training is generally not what they're going to receive in most present-day aikido dojos.

If I weren't concerned with effective technique, I'd be doing weightlifting and yoga instead, as they certainly increase longevity and one's standard of living without many of the injuries and training risks associated with martial arts.

So, I was stuck on the idea of being able to defeat someone without really fighting, without ever getting your hands dirty, without having to ever resort to brute force. Such an enticing proposition could be realized and achieved, I firmly believed, through hard, consistent training, training that I would have to endure as an uchideshi, that I somehow knew I wasn't getting through regular classes, despite maintaining a weekly three to five day training schedule.

Just as neuromuscular memory was achieved in judo through uchikomi, where you would drill the initial movement or phase of a throw until it was an instantaneous reaction, I knew I needed to "drill" the blending movements of aikido. Since I hadn't found that aikido used highly repetitive drills for specific movements or portions of movements, I figured I would ingrain the aiki movements into my body by simply increasing the volume of training.

That had to be the answer, because so far, things weren't adding up. It's a very uncomfortable feeling when your expected effectiveness does not align with your actual result. How are you to honestly assess and pinpoint exactly where the problem lies? Do you doubt yourself, doubt the techniques, or doubt the training method? It's a tough one to figure out on your own, especially if the instruction you're receiving doesn't honestly address real-life resistance levels.

Eric was a friend of mine I got together with to train in Brazilian Jiu-Jitsu. He had a wrestling background and a smattering of BJJ. I can't think of anything I was able to pull off in sparring that I learned in aikido class, only my judo background saved me from total annihilation. So what was going on here? I chose to doubt the training method and myself. The solution, I thought, was to train more often and with more intensity, that was the secret to making aikido "work."

Additionally, on the nights Ken would teach aikido at Aikido North, we would do an exercise modeled after henka (variations) in Seibukan Jujutsu. Someone would make a strong attack of their choosing, and the defender could use any defense they liked, as long as safety and control were maintained. If the techniques the defender was trying to execute were not immediately effective, the attacker could move into something else.

I observed that as soon as people were given the OK to even mildly resist the techniques, the overcommitted nature of their attacks dried up and what seemed to work consistently were hip throws from Judo followed by Brazilian Jiu-Jitsu groundwork. The question is, what would I have done if I hadn't had a background in other martial arts?

Now I can at least be honest with myself and admit that although I was a deeply dedicated student, and had excellent instructors, hardly anything I had learned would have worked in the street against an experienced fighter. The movements off the line of attack were excellent, but if a 250-pound construction worker wanted to teach me a lesson, I would have died if I had to depend solely on the physical skills and knowledge I had gained from aikido. Without a doubt.

This is something I had to come to grips with over a long period of time. I'm a believer by nature. I like to check, investigate, analyze, research, and dissect arts and their techniques, but basically, I'm optimistic during the process and I give them the benefit of the doubt. So I believed, and I trained, and what I learned during that time has served me well, but I can't bring myself to invest any more time in it now that I know the variety of training one must undergo in order to be a complete, well-rounded martial artist.

Had I heard my own arguments a few years ago, I would have simply dismissed them as a bitter rant from an unenlightened, unskilled practitioner. After all, if I were good enough, it would work, just as it worked for Morihei Ueshiba and his top students, including Mochizuki, Tomiki, Shioda, and Tohei. So why did their stuff work while mine didn't?

I think it comes down to hard training. Hard training in a "hard" style. I mean, O'Sensei didn't learn aikido, he learned Daito-Ryu Aiki-Jujutsu, and his early students also learned razor-sharp aiki-jujutsu techniques. What I learned was aikido, the end product of a successful experiment where Morihei

Ueshiba filtered an old battlefield art into something else, a unique approach that reflected his philosophy, but that wasn't what I was looking for. I liked the philosophy, but unfortunately, the techniques served as a metaphor for the philosophy, and they weren't working for me. I was looking for aiki-jujutsu; I was looking for the hard training. I wanted to learn what those masters had learned, without it being diluted or removed from its source.

It's difficult coming from a traditional background, where it's generally considered impolite to honestly question or probe too deeply without already having a high rank, to then study an art steeped in mysticism, because it can cast a spell over the students and practitioners. This aiki-enchantment can create a quasi cult like atmosphere for those who buy into the belief system. Don't get me wrong, I'm not calling an aikido class a cult, but it is a belief system, and there is certainly a kind of rift between those that believe in it's magic and those that do not. I've felt this division, because I was one of the most faithful adherents of the art.

When I came to study Seibukan Jujutsu, I didn't really have any expectations. I knew that Sensei would have what I was looking for, after all, he was a yondan (fourth degree black belt) in aikido at the time. I wasn't exactly sure what he was doing teaching jujutsu, but I knew that because he really understood this art I had fallen in love with, I believed he knew what was best.

I knew we had similar viewpoints about the strict "time in" system of certain martial arts. The aikido association we were affiliated through required a certain number of training hours to be marked down before you were eligible for your next belt, with testing every six months or so. Over the course of two devoted years, I rose only two ranks, up from sixth kyu to fourth, which was rapid for my dojo. While the minimum time requirement for shodan was five years of consistent training, I simply couldn't rationalize how the technical skills one would possess after receiving his Shodan could merit a five-year commitment. It ate away at me, but I kept my mouth shut because it wasn't my place to say anything. After all, I was just a yonkyu. But I saw students who had been training for seven to ten years, and still had not received their shodan.

Years before I had begun training, Sensei had flown up to Alaska and given a seminar at Aikido North. During that weekend, one of the young female students asked Sensei how long it would take him to bring someone up to shodan. He looked at her calmly and said, "About three months." Needless to say, everyone was shocked. I'm sure it offended some, and others may have dismissed him, but when I heard that story, I concurred wholeheartedly.

In some arts it does take five to seven years (or more!) of hard consistent training to receive your black belt, but generally those are arts where you test your skills in sparring against uncooperative, equally skilled opponents. Usually, it takes that long to build and combine the attributes and technical proficiency of a "black belt" in a particular system. The ironic thing is, it's sometimes possible to progress faster in arts like this because you have an opportunity to display your attributes and experience, resulting in rapid promotion if deserved. If you're a white belt in Brazilian Jiu-Jitsu and are tapping out blue belts, the instructor will note that and get the situation adjusted, instead of forcing you to wait for a mandatory six-month period, X'ing off the boxes next to your name, making sure your hours are counted. You really get a chance to display your skills, instead of having to bite your lip as people who couldn't survive a bar brawl point out how your technique is incorrect.

But there's no sparring in aikido, no uncooperative opponents, and little chance to display your attributes. So you put your time in, but I've come to think that the whole "time-in" system that can be terribly unfair to those that may deserve more rapid promotion, particularly if they're hungry, motivated, and talented. Look at Jerry Bohlander, he spends six months training at the Lion's Den, enters the UFC, has a successful outing, and proves that time in, as the lone indicator of proficiency, is false. Frank Shamrock is another example. In a period of five years, he went from never having studied a martial art to becoming the King of Pancrase and an undisputed Ultimate Fighting Champion. Or, in that same period of time, he could've gotten his shodan in aikido.

Something in me rebels against the "set-in-stone" time in policies of many dojos and martial arts organizations. Saying that it takes seven years to earn your black belt, no exceptions, is a really close-minded, oppressive method more akin to martial incarceration than education. Even our school systems allow the exceptional to be appropriately placed. If it takes 7 to 10 years to develop the skills of black belt, as it does in some arts, that's great, and you shouldn't be promoted ahead of time. But not acknowledging physical prowess gained through previous martial experience, drawing out the process simply to keep students in enrollment, or to keep an ego buffer between the rank of the students and sensei is simply wrong.

It's not necessarily about the time you've served, it's what you make of it. Time is not experience, and it's the quality of your martial experience that makes the difference.

Sensei certainly allowed me to make the most of my time as an uchideshi. From the beginning, he sensed that I was in a box, trapped in my own aiki mentality. But instead of giving unsolicited thoughts and opinions, he prefers to have people form their own opinions and make their own choices. Therefore, he sought to expose me to different aspects of the martial arts, expanding my consciousness through an increased knowledge base. He took me to an aiki-jujutsu seminar of Yanagi-Ryu Soke Don Angier; I accompanied him several times to the Redwood city dojo of his aikido instructor, Frank Doran; he allowed me to study Brazilian Jiu-Jitsu under Claudio Franca; and he answered all my questions, which were never in short supply.

Sensei had been an uchideshi three different times at aikido's hombu dojo in Iwama, Japan. As head instructor, Saito Sensei is reputed as being the closest technical representation of Morihei Ueshiba. Through hard years of being both an uchideshi and a teacher, I knew Saito would have to be the one that could make aikido "work," the way I envisioned it working in a physical confrontation.

So I asked the question I had been dying to know the answer to for years. I had always felt sheepish about asking such things in a really traditional setting, but now that I had a resource who could give me a qualified answer, I couldn't pass up the opportunity. How would Saito Sensei, arguably the most proficient aikido practitioner alive, fare in the UFC? Would he, through the severity of his training and years of experience, be able to blend in that imperceptible fraction of a second where his opponent would be off balance? Would he be able to execute ikkyo through yonkyo, an iriminage, or a kotegaeshi?

Sensei's answer was what I had both waited for and feared. He told me, in no uncertain terms, that Saito would be demolished. It didn't matter that he was the best in the world at his particular style, when it came to fighting the guys in the UFC, he'd be dead. Then I asked about the mystical Morihei Ueshiba, and whether or not he would fare well. Sensei looked at me and said, "Are you kidding? Against somebody like Kimo? If they fought, Kimo would be the new O'Sensei!"

We laughed, but part of me winced when I heard this, and a little bit of my innocence, the part that wants to believe in magic and miracles, died right then. Really, deep down, I knew the answer before I asked. I was just lying to myself. Or maybe not even lying, but choosing to not look at what experience had already shown me. Growing up hurts, the truth hurts, but ultimately it serves you better as I knew that I was finally discovering answers to questions I needed to know. It's hard to let an emotional investment go, but I realized it was better to ride out my disillusionment now than later, or after I had invested a year as an uchideshi in an aikido dojo as I had originally planned.

Although I still agreed with the philosophy of aikido, and I loved the aesthetic beauty of the circular movements, I wasn't taking martial arts classes to simply look pretty or philosophize. I wanted to learn concrete, physical skills that would serve me if they were ever put to the test. After all, I was 21, a young buck, ready to make the most of the energetic reservoir that can dissipate with age. I had no time to waste, and I knew that the style I chose had to be efficient and effective. Good techniques, well rounded, to provide both a good base of knowledge and a healthy perspective on martial arts. I thought aikido was what I wanted, but slowly realized that Seibukan was closer to my disposition.

I generally take issue with the aikido I've learned, seen, and come in contact with being advertised as self-defense. Although there are aspects and techniques of aikido that I believe can be gleaned and added to your martial arsenal (i.e. footwork for getting off the line, blending with an overcommitted attack, etc.), I could never recommend it to somebody who wanted to quickly learn self-defense. Not only is there too much silence about what works and what doesn't, the non-competitive training method doesn't put students in pressure situations close enough to real confrontations, breeding a false sense of security in students through affirmations such as:

1. It may take 20 years, but this stuff will work if you just keep practicing.

2. Don't worry about strength, since physical conditioning isn't that important.

3. These exercises we're doing are how attacks really are.

4. If it's not working, you're not using your center.

5. Keep extending that ki (energy) to keep him at bay!

It's not fair to your students to misrepresent what your art is capable of. If your average aikido student rolled with a judo or Brazilian Jiu-Jitsu player, or got in the ring with a boxer or kickboxer, he wouldn't know what to do with that kind of intensity. He'd simply be overwhelmed. I've seen this point debated through letters to the editor in Aikido Today Magazine, but there's only one way to find out. Do it. To paraphrase Bruce Lee, you can't learn to swim unless you get wet, so how can you learn how to fight without fighting?

I remember an aikidoka, who was very good, tell me that he could probably slip any punch thrown at him. At the time, I believed him, but now with more experience, I disagree. He probably could have slipped any punch thrown at him if it was telegraphed, traveled in a straight line, and was done in a method identical to our practice in class. But there are boxers with hands so quick that you'd be in the middle of processing the thought, "I think it's coming," and next thing you know, you're on the floor. And that's without fakes, mixing levels, or combinations.

Now there are styles that are quite hard, such as Yoshinkan, and instructors who have kept closer to the roots of aikido, where my arguments aren't really applicable. Aikido is actually a very general word, I've come to find out, and there are tons of styles and instructors that are hard, soft, or somewhere in the middle. As Toshishiro Obata expressed in his book <u>Samurai Aiki-jutsu</u>, he sometimes feels embarrassed watching soft-style aikido demonstrations, and considers it an insult to the legacy of both Sokaku Takeda and Morihei Ueshiba. He is a vocal advocate of aikido and its combat effectiveness, but he practices a hard style derived from hard training as an uchideshi under Gozo Shioda, who in turn studied under O'Sensei during his physical prime. Because of that generational progression, hard training under masters in their prime, the masculine essence of Daito-Ryu Aiki-Jujutsu has been preserved.

Strong, simple, direct, practical. Seagal, Obata, Koga, and plenty of other instructors keep these points in mind, and consequently, their aikido is very applicable to self-defense. But when the emphasis changes from martial to art, then those who are looking for the former and settle for the latter are really shortchanged, and a disservice has been rendered.

In all fairness, modern-day aikido tries to do something different by using the aiki movements as an analogy for conflict resolution and non-violence. It's a tired argument, but the escalation of interpersonal violence will always end with the guy with a bomb in his backpack. Hand-to-hand combat leads to a stick or knife fight, a stick or knife will lead to guns, guns lead to larger guns, and eventually the guy with the bomb in his backpack who's going to "get you back," regardless of the cost, is the ultimate warrior. The terrorist wins if you play that game, but aikido strives for a different path. It's a martial philosophy that serves both its practitioners and humanity in general, but I feel the message is somehow weakened when the preparation for war that insures the peace is reduced to a shell of what's actually necessary.

I believe that if the spiritual and mental benefits traditionally derived from training, (increased self-confidence, inner peace, etc...) are over-intellectualized, and the by-products of training become the focal point, you should be taking a self-empowerment seminar instead of a martial art. Focus on the physical, and under the proper instruction, everything will come in time. Over-intellectualization can kill an art.

This is probably disturbing to many readers, particularly if they're aikido practitioners or instructors. But despite all I've said, I still love aikido. It's a beautiful art, it's lots of fun to train in, I love the people it attracts, and there's a kind of "aiki-high" that becomes addictive as practitioners take each other's balance with proper timing. Besides, some people don't care if their art is effective or not. It may be fun, it may get them out of the house or provide them with an excuse to meet up with their friends. Whatever the reason, my position is irrelevant to this particular demographic.

So who am I writing this chapter for? I'm writing it for the kid who goes straight to the martial arts section of a bookstore, who shows up early for training and loiters afterward, and is insatiably hungry for knowledge and experience in a way most adults can barely remember.

I'm writing it for the kid who's going to reread this book, in order to bring the documented experiences closer to home. I'm aiming this at the kid I was, because I know he's out there, and what I've written is what I would have liked to have known ahead of time. Stand on my shoulders, as I've stood on the shoulders of others, and let my experience save you a couple of steps, putting you a few feet ahead of the learning curve.

For the general reader or martial artist, my aim was to stimulate you into thinking honestly about the art you're practicing and its limitations. Most instructors, having been in martial arts for years and worked with thousands of bodies, know that some techniques will not work on some people, and you have to be tough to win a fight if your opponent is formidable in the least. Some pass on this information, others keep it quiet. If you were a beginner, what would you want to know?

It wasn't fun leaving this box, but I'm better for it. Changing from a devout, subjective view to a disillusioned, but more objective perspective on aikido has been one of the most painful experiences I've ever had in the martial arts. However, climbing out has made me grow tremendously, and now I'm able to nod, smile, and offer encouragement as the newly initiated proselytize about how karate, ninjitsu, Brazilian Jiu-Jitsu, or tae kwon do is the best.

And they're 100 percent right. They are the best. The best art for them at that moment because they're enthusiastic and determined to succeed. At that point, everybody wins.

Later, the box you've chosen to enter may begin closing in on you. Aikido, Seibukan, Brazilian Jiu-Jitsu, the parameters of each art form a box technically in its structure and mentally within its practitioners. As martial artists, we must strive to transcend styles, and overcome our weaknesses. As human beings, we must seek to work through the categories that separate us, and our self-imposed limitations. It takes work, and none of this can happen without a certain amount of analysis and unbiased reflection. What are you choosing to believe, what are you buying into, what are you suppressing because it may not fit with your paradigm of the world?

It's not easy, but it's our obligation to take an honest look at ourselves, step outside our comfort zone, beyond the world we know, and climb out of the box. Who better to do it than a martial artist? After all, isn't that what all this warrior training is for?

AN HONEST DRAW

I never really liked iaido, but I did it anyway.

After receiving my green belt in Seibukan, Sensei told me I could train in one of the additional arts taught at the academy. Iaido and ninjitsu were my options, and it took some serious mulling over to make a decision.

I didn't really choose iaido as much as decide against ninjitsu. It seemed to me that ninjitsu had a lot of, for lack of a better term, dark energy surrounding it. Running around in black suits, tossing throwing stars- there was a little too much make believe in it for my taste. Plus, some of the practitioners I had run into had an ego trip that broadcast this message:

"You don't know the secrets I know. Mess with me and I'll kill you. I am a ninja!"

I didn't want to get involved in that. Those guys would hurt me.

That isn't to say that make believe isn't involved in iaido. Nobody walks around with a sword these days, so if the question of practical value pops up, push it back down because it's really nil.

Devotees will attest that much can be learned from the sword. I can agree with this. From energy extension, body coordination, and mental focus to simply strengthening up your wrists, the sword can offer much as a training tool, but you have to practice. A lot.

Hour after hour must be put in before you can start reaping practical by-products of sword training, and personally, I'd rather spend that time kicking the heavy bag or doing arm bar drills.

Sensei gave me a private introductory lesson on how to use, wear, draw, and bow with the sword. This was necessary. In my first encounter with the weapon, I was clumsy and dangerous. Half the time my sword was falling out of the saya (scabbard), and the other half was spent stabbing myself, trying to put it back in.

I must say, though, it was a good discipline. Wednesdays were my long days at the dojo, starting with the kids' classes in the afternoon, usually training through the breaks until the seven o'clock class. After that was finished, we had iaido until nine thirty at night. I was always fading halfway through class, running low on blood sugar and irritability increasing. After iaido was finished, I would clean and oil Sensei's sword and the dojo sword I was using, then put them both away. Finally, having swung for my supper, I allowed myself to eat.

But bearing discomfort isn't the kind of discipline that iaido is all about. The real work with the sword is being able to honestly assess where you are. I'm not just talking about class, I mean in all areas of your life. It starts with the sword, then if practiced properly, spills into other activities.

From the outside, iaido is ridiculously simple. Draw the sword, maybe do a few cuts, then put it back. It looks pretty, you can make a cool sound if you cut the air properly, but it doesn't seem like the stuff that could make a dent in your daily life. Hey, where's The Work?

It's in the details. First, iaido is a solo activity, which means you don't have to listen to anybody else if you don't want to. In jujutsu, a partner can force you to listen to him by physically proving that your technique doesn't work if done improperly. In iaido, that isn't the case. If you want to draw your sword so fast that you bend it, swing with your arms and not your body, or sheathe it as ingloriously as it was freed, you can. Instructors and peers may offer advice, but the burden is on the student to trust in the criticism, then correct and improve. If you want to just let the words go by and continue bad habits, there's nothing and no one to stop you.

Some methods are better than others, and it may be ugly, but if you can yank that thing out and shove it back in, it's swordsmanship. It may not be good, or as effective as it could be, but it works. That, however, is not iaido. That's something else entirely.

Iaido is constantly striving to better yourself by monitoring and improving every aspect of drawing, cutting, and sheathing the sword. It's hard to do, continually searching for things to improve upon, not allowing yourself to rest on your laurels. Most people don't consciously believe that they're choosing to stagnate, but they do, since it's the default result of not integrating criticism into improvement.

There's always something to work on with the sword, and iaido will train you to look intently for where The Work is needed. It won't fix anything by itself, but it may prepare you to look deeper into your own life, and challenge you to examine the most fundamental attitudes you hold. One of the most uncomfortable discoveries I've found began with ironing out the physical flaws in my swordwork, then continuing that level of hyper-awareness and scrutiny to question a very personal facet: my own honesty.

I like to think of myself as an honest person, but it's pretty easy to be honest with others. If you're not, there are consequences when the lies are cut and the truth is known. But what about being honest with yourself? No one can call you on that except you.

I took a look at myself and realized that I lie all the time. Not necessarily in an overt manner, but at the very least by mental omission. Choosing not to think of my mess-ups, the trouble I've caused others, things I've said that should have never left my lips, awkward moments and segments of my life; in short, all the things that I gloss over because they're uncomfortable.

I'm not recommending that you dwell on the past, but I think it's necessary to learn lessons from the moments you enjoy least, so the fear of bringing up the past won't hold you from progressing in the future.

It's agonizingly simple: Can you be honest with yourself? Are you willing to listen to criticism and acknowledge those problem areas? Are you able to assess where you're at and work through your problems, instead of burying them or running away? Can you acknowledge things from your past that you thought you'd left behind, or hoped you'd never have to dredge up again?

I'd like to look away during those times of discomfort, but I know that's not going to serve me in the long run. I think those key seconds of acknowledgement or dismissal can define who you are as an individual. Which path will you travel by? Can you eat bitter now and trust in the sweet?

If you can, you will grow, improve, excel, and transcend. If you can't, you will remain, cajoling yourself, resting on a plateau. So as much as I dislike iaido, I must admit, it helps you do The Work. It may not be easy, but I don't think internal evaluations can ever be. I'm trying to eat bitter, be honest, and to do the right thing, but it's seldom the easy option. I don't even like doing it, but I know I'll be better off down the road.

I guess I'll do it anyway.

A LESSON IN HUMILITY

My first experience with Brazilian Jiu Jitsu was probably the same as most people in the country: watching Royce Gracie demolish the competition in UFC 2.

With my judo experience, I knew what he was doing with the armbars and chokes, and I was fascinated with his strategy as questions about different martial arts were being visually answered. My friends basically said, "Oh my God," and sat there, dumbfounded at the reality of fighting.

They had thought it was going to look like an adrenalized, choreographed fight scene from a movie, and to some extent, so had I. What we're exposed to is what we expect, and movies can certainly shape expectations in the minds of the uninitiated.

Now, with mixed martial art competitions booming and exposure increasing, people may expect a physical altercation to be like an MMA match, but will again be surprised at what a street fight is really like. Friends, boots, weapons, asphalt, bottles, teeth, the element of surprise, and merciless brutality are some of the variables that make street fights as eye-opening as the UFC was to movie magic.

Still, it answered a lot of questions for me. As a teenager, I had originally bought into the appearance of martial demonstrations as combat reality. I had witnessed some counter-indications to these well-crafted illusions, but wasn't entirely sure of where to place them or how they fit into my mystical martial arts paradigm. I certainly understand how it fits together now, but then, with little or no guidance, I could only file the experiences away.

While in Canada, my buddy and I taught a self-defense class after school. He passed on information from years of karate training, and I taught basic judo throws. One day I found myself sparring in the class, point karate style, with a guy who was stronger, more experienced, much more aggressive, and generally a tough SOB. He was killing me.

Something had to change, so I dove in, grabbed his gi, and did a hip throw to take him to the ground. I remember thinking, "My God, he's like a fish out of water." This guy who was a stud on his feet was suddenly very easy to control, with only the most basic ground skills in my repertoire. I internalized that experience and filed it away.

Later that year a teacher at the school approached me and mentioned he had seen us working out in our uniforms. He asked if it would it be permissible to join us for judo, and mentioned that he already had some experience. "Sure," I said, and that afternoon we worked out for the first time. He dressed in an unbleached gi and a yellow belt he'd dyed himself, and we began, beginning with stretching and a warm up, moving into uchikomi (partial, repetitive throwing motions), and proceeded to randori (sparring).

Well, when it came to randori, he was impossible to throw. To my surprise, he tossed me around easily, and not necessarily with traditional judo techniques.

Granted, I was lighter, but it was such a shock to be manhandled so skillfully by this stranger. I asked him about his past, and he told me how he wrestled through high school, college, and then in international competition. We trained a few more sessions and got along well.

One thing we discussed was the striker versus the grappler. "Yah," he said, "he may be able to get me with a punch, but he better make it good because as soon as I get a hold of him, it's over." I also found this curious, but again, could only file it away, because I didn't really understand how to categorize the information that had just been given. I was, however, getting an inkling of how important ground skills were.

Again, this happened before my exposure to the UFC, and before the importance of ground grappling was widely believed or supported. Now, of course, cross-training and ground grappling are viewed as mandatory for serious martial artists. Brazilian Jiu-Jitsu was a wake-up call to the martial arts community, and my physical introduction to the art was equally shocking, beginning with a chance encounter on the Internet.

I was surfing the net, and went to one of my bookmarked sites, Tim Mousel's Brazilian Jiu Jitsu discussion forum. Glancing at the posts, I saw one requesting a training partner in Anchorage, Alaska. I hadn't ever seen anything like this before in my neck of the woods, so I e-mailed him immediately and told him what my martial arts background was. He wrote back, satisfied I wasn't a mindless bruiser, and excited about the possibility of a new training partner. Apparently, his instructor had been a local character named Felix, a Gracie Jiu Jitsu fanatic who had gone around to local dojos offering unsolicited challenges.

Felix once came into Aikido North, and told me after watching a class, "You know this stuff doesn't work. All you need is grappling and boxing." I smiled and nodded, but was surprised at the nerve of him actually coming into a dojo to insult the art. He was waiting for Ken to finish teaching the class, so he could roll around with him. I told Felix that Ken was good, and he agreed. "Yes, Ken is good, but I am better now." He went on, confident his new techniques would give him the winning edge.

Ken was never against playing with guys from different arts, and consequently had to field challenges from time to time. But on this night, Ken couldn't play because strict instructions had been left by the head instructor to not have people on the mat who weren't affiliated with the dojo, instructions specifically tailored for our friend. So Felix left disappointed, with no one to play with that night.

Nor could Felix train with Eric, my new friend. Initially, he taught Eric and awarded him his blue belt, but apparently didn't handle it well when Eric began consistently tapping him out. As he put it, Felix had not yet learned the "humble spirit," so Eric left, scrounging training partners wherever he could, whether through work, friends, or advertisement.

Eric's last training partner, an old friend, reacted poorly to a mata leao ("Lion Killing" in Portuguese), also known as a rear strangle. Eric, sinking the choke and expecting a tap, felt fists hitting his face as his friend, in a mix of anger and desperation, swung backwards and over his head. Eric, realizing that this was not a tap, and this was probably not the time for him to release his hold, sat back and relaxed. His friend eventually calmed down, but clearly, this was the last training session.

Now he had a new training partner: me. We set up a time to get together on Sunday after the open mat training session at Aikido North. I was really excited about being able to spar and hopefully make a new friend in the process, but that morning as I shared my enthusiasm with my fellow aikido students, describing how I met this guy over the Internet, I watched their faces change. Let's just say they weren't as hot on the idea as I was. Nevertheless, they wished me the best of luck and told me to give them a report on how it went.

Eric and I met at a public recreational center on the other side of town that Sunday afternoon. He stood 5 feet 10 inches at 160 pounds, with dirty blond hair, but you could tell he was a wrestler by his sinewy frame. We paid the fee at the front desk and went upstairs to lay down the mats. Getting dressed, we both put on our uniforms, he with a blue belt, I with my white.

There was some preliminary warming up and stretching, then he went over some basic positions: the guard, mount, sidemount. Thus, having gone through the obligatory preparations, we were ready to spar.

Eric had mentioned that he liked to go at maximum exertion levels during his training, to keep the realism high. He also conceded that this probably contributed to the high burnout rate of his training partners. I knew that this would be pretty intense, but it was what both of us wanted, and we were itching to "get it on," so to speak.

We began at opposite ends of the mat, with our stylistic differences exemplified. He adopted a wrestler's crouch, elbows in, with rounded back; I remained upright, arms open, the natural posture of Kodokan Judo. We circled, not quite close enough for me to grab his gi, and eyed each other warily. Suddenly, he shot in, and although I tried to sprawl, it was incomplete. With a fistful of my gi bottom (as I hopped to retain my balance), Eric tenaciously fought for the other leg and took me to the ground.

Immediately I went to the guard, but somehow, in a chaotic flurry of activity, he passed my guard, achieved sidemount, and was on his way to mounting me. Logically, I knew that you should NEVER give your opponent your back, but for some reason, in a combination of habit and instinct, I rolled over to my elbows and knees.

Turtled up in this position, the limbs are kept in to protect against joint locks, chin tucked down and hands crossed, palms pressed out around my neck to prevent chokes. This is usually a good position in competition judo, where if you can guard against a strong attack unlikely to end in a quick submission, the referee will stand you up. There are other defenses from this position, but that's only if your opponent's objective is to put your back on the ground for the pin or immobilization.

But on this day, there was no time limits, referee, or objective to pin. Eric felt me roll over, put the hooks in, and pushing his hips forward to arch my back, exposed my neck. He filled the gap between my chin and chest with the crook of his elbow, and the choke was sunk. Valiantly, I tapped.

That first match took less than 30 seconds. Although the rest of the matches that day would often last longer, the positions of tapper and tappee would remain consistent. I did lots of things that make me cringe when I think about them now: giving my back, not realizing the importance of moving my hips, and trying to choke while I was within Eric's guard. Although I did get him in one armbar, I must have tapped more than 25 times that afternoon, to the point of mutual exhaustion. We promised to train the next week, same time, same place, with the six days in-between sessions needed to heal my wounds.

I went over to a friend's house afterward, and after taking one look at me, he asked, "What happened? It looks like you got your ass kicked!" I smiled, and told him where I'd been, though the scratches, scrapes, and abrasions suffered during training probably looked worse than they felt. In particular, the left side of my face had a huge raspberry; another wound impossible to pinpoint from the chaos of maximal exertion. As for the people at Aikido North, they just shook their heads.

We continued to train in subsequent months, and I ended up getting Chris involved, but unfortunately the other training partners we tried to recruit would either be inconsistent or, more commonly, simply no shows.

No matter, we trained on, with the submission ratio eventually turning to 60-40, but still in Eric's favor.

Eric lost this training partner when I moved down to Monterey to become an uchideshi, and I didn't think I would have a chance at all to wrestle around since I was living in a classical jujutsu dojo. But, as fate would have it, I was sweeping the mat before class (not an unusual activity for one in my position), and struck up a conversation with the woman pushing a broom next to me.

At that time, I still didn't know more than a handful of people in the dojo. Carolynn, as she introduced herself to me, began talking about the no-holds-barred event Extreme Fighting III, which she had just seen that weekend at her friend's house. Hearing this, and having resigned myself to be out of the no-holds-barred fighting loop, with little or no access to that kind of information, I was ecstatic.

I peppered her with questions, most of which she couldn't give answers to, as she was helping out in the kitchen for most of the show. I started naming off different fighters she probably saw, and she did remember that Conan Silviera had lost to a black kickboxer, later revealed to be Maurice Smith. Flabbergasted, I begged her to get a copy of the tape, which she promised she would deliver.

Later, as Carolynn and I developed our friendship, she told me of her martial arts history, which included two black belts in different forms of Hapkido, and of her training in Brazilian Jiu Jitsu under Claudio Franca, a four-time state, three-time Brazilian, and two-time Pan-American champion.

We set up a training time after class where she taught me the basics of BJJ as she had learned them, and then had her friend Michael come to the dojo and give me a lesson, which included sparring. Michael, a hulking man on a 6 foot frame, was an old training partner of Carolynn's in Hapkido, and they once again met up at Claudio's. Michael was an enormous BJJ fan, having spent time training in Torrance under the Gracies, and was the only other person I had met that was as captivated by the UFC and no-holds-barred fighting events as I was. We trained that day and I was once again annihilated. He did, however, think I'd enjoy training at Claudio's, and recommended beginning if I had the opportunity.

Carolynn had told me, quite explicitly, that if I were to study the art, it shouldn't be under anyone other than Claudio, because he was one of the few authentic BJJ instructors around in our area. She wanted me to meet him, so we drove up to Santa Cruz on a Friday night (the only night during the week I wasn't obligated to train) and participated in his class.

Claudio was 175 pounds and six feet tall, with a muscular physique, devoid of visible fat. A heavy Portuguese accent and a firm handshake warmly greeted me, "Hoy, my friend, how are you?" Claudio made sure I lived through the first class (at that time, the warm-ups were Olympian), and let me roll with his top American student, Garth Taylor. Overall, I enjoyed it thoroughly, and believed my exposure to Claudio's dojo was no accident.

I was anxious to begin training, but first had to secure permission from Sensei. Friday night is the time he taught ninjitsu at the dojo, and was generally a day of rest for me. I was willing to give up that day to augment my training with ground grappling once a week, but had no idea whether Sensei would agree to this.

I knew it wouldn't distract me from my regular training (which was in no short supply), and I felt both safe in Claudio's dojo and comfortable under his instruction. If there had been any usual or particularly unsettling vibes, I wouldn't have even entertained the thought.

Sensei himself, with his ranks in aikido, jujutsu, ninjitsu, and karate, obviously believed in cross-training and in being a martial artist, rather than a particular stylist. On the other hand, I had committed myself to a year focusing exclusively on Seibukan, so I could understand if he believed it would take away focus from the main art, and he certainly didn't want me getting hurt at an unfamiliar dojo.

I consulted others on what approach I should take. I plotted hypothetical dialogues and prepared persuasive arguments. Some suggested that since I was a green belt at the time, I should center my pitch on having access to all the principles for the level of shodan, or on the fact that it wouldn't be an entirely new activity, but rather a continuation of my Alaskan masochism.

Finally, I shelved all approaches, and just told him, straight out, that I wanted to supplement my training by going to Santa Cruz on Friday nights. I also told him that although I felt that this would be a positive experience, whatever he said, yes or no, I would not protest his decision. I knew that Sensei, being responsible for all aspects of my training, was sincerely looking out for my best interests. He listened to me, very carefully, and said he would have an answer next Thursday, one week away.

Well, Thursday came and went with no answer. Sensei probably had an answer, but I knew deep down that if I bugged him, I would probably ruin it. I kept my mouth shut and waited for him to offer a decision.

Another week went by and I was dying inside, I really wanted to know what he thought about it, but something inside told me, "Well Roy, here's your chance to practice non-attachment and letting go."

I thought that non-attachment had been a strong suit of mine. In fact, it naturally arose from situations I didn't care about. From that perspective, it's easy to think of yourself as a logical, disciplined being, unswayed by petty emotions. There aren't that many things in my life that really inspire passionate devotion: Martial arts, the UFC, women and music. But overall, I'm even keeled.

The problem was, I was now learning firsthand how difficult non-attachment is to actually practice when it's something you want very badly. Now I get why Gandhi would sleep next to naked devotees to test his willpower. It's another level of control and discipline, and I actually wouldn't mind replicating that experiment for my own personal development.

But for now, I having enough of a problem just keeping my mouth shut and letting Sensei make the first move. Finally, the next week, I was talking to Sensei in the dojo's tatami room, and he said he had an answer. This took me totally by surprise since the conversation wasn't even near that subject. He began:

"I've given it a lot of thought, and traditionally, an uchideshi is forbidden to engage in training outside of the dojo, because the objective is to focus on the understanding of one art under the guidance of a master."

I nodded, understanding how he arrived at his decision, and a bit relieved for finally receiving an answer, even though it wasn't the one I wanted. Then he continued:

"But I'm into breaking tradition. So this will be an experiment and we'll see how it goes. I don't know, you may have come down from Alaska to make a connection with this teacher, just as you've made this connection with me, and I want to help guide you. So yes, you can go to Santa Cruz and study Brazilian Jiu Jitsu."

I was happy. Very happy. Either way would have been fine, but I'll be honest: I like it when things go my way. And even though I didn't learn the hard lesson that time, I learned about letting go of outcomes in situations that I have little or no control over.

Brazilian Jiu Jitsu has helped me in Seibukan, and Seibukan has assisted me in learning BJJ. First off, there is an emphasis in Seibukan on principles, rather than on techniques, which allows a more thorough understanding of what makes the techniques work. A thorough understanding of principles gives students the opportunity to be creative and look for new or innovative ways of entering techniques, keeping an art fresh.

I believe in classical training, because many of the requirements and exercises in these older arts can help further the range and skills of a martial artist, even if they aren't directly applicable to winning a fight. I see this in a variety of subtle ways, but ukemi springs to mind as a good example. I've found that it's more often practiced , and more heavily stressed, in older judo and jujutsu traditions, and I haven't seen this kind of time devotion and emphasis in their modern derivations, such as BJJ. Why?

One reason is that in a competition, no one's going to tap to good ukemi, no matter how polished or practical it may be. Still, there are benefits in it, ranging from real-life falling skills to enhanced kinesthetic awareness.

So, the benefits of these specialized skills may often be masked or unseen in a martial arena, but other art forms make it easier to realize the benefits of traditional training. Whether it's exhibited in an electric guitar solo or modern dance performance, the advantage of a classical base can often be spotted through the precision of technique in both music and dance, because of the specific physical demands inherent in classical guitar or the discipline of ballet. Also, Chopin and Paganini may not be dominating the current music scene, but that doesn't mean there's no worth in what they've created.

Studying, practicing, and finally understanding this music can give a student a tremendous amount of perspective on more contemporary creations, in addition to expanding and improving technical ability. A understanding of what has gone before can enhance your perspective on why the old was altered to form what's now the new.

BJJ has helped my classical training as well. Seibukan is a highly technical art, but the more time that's spent on learning and perfecting new techniques, the less time there is for developing the attributes that make techniques effective.

I remember doing knuckle push-ups in Tae Kwon Do class, thinking ,"What are we doing? I didn't come here for this!" I went there for technical instruction in kicking, not upper-body conditioning, so I can partially agree that the emphasis should be on martial techniques, not on attribute development, when I go to class. If I wanted to get stronger, I can do that on my own time, and often do.

However, there is something in the group dynamic of mass calisthenics that pushes you a lot farther than doing them at home in front of the tube. Also, not everybody works out on their own, so sometimes the only chance a person may have to develop speed and strength is at the dojo during a few weekly training hours. But that is the nature of Seibukan. The techniques are there, but it's up to you to bring them to life through individualized attribute training.

In addition, sparring is consistently a large part of a BJJ class. In Seibukan, there is no sparring, only henka (variations). Henka is an exercise to improve coordination, timing, matching energy levels and spontaneity, as two training partners do random attacks, and variations on previously learned techniques are used to defend. But the level of resistance is never the same, and not intended to be the same, as a skilled opponent trying to submit you and you doing the same to them.

The ability to remain mentally calm during sparring in BJJ or Judo while expending great amounts of energy is a martial virtue developed through practice. Sparring, at its roughest, is still only 80 to 90 percent of the adrenalized frenzy experienced in a street fight, but pushing that window of familiar exertion does something very practical and necessary. It expands the practitioner's ability to "turn it on" and increase the intensity; or "tone it down," and simply match the energy level of the attack.

As my old judo coach told me, "Once you've been tortured by masters, nothing else phases you anymore." I agree. After you've been choked mercilessly, had your joints locked out at full speed and power, been smothered, suffocated, and generally maligned, the tendency to panic as people are rushing in to grab or strike you diminishes. Consequently, control during Seibukan exercises such as henka and tai sabaki increases in relation to your ability to keep cool.

Finally, BJJ keeps you humble. Classical jujutsu and aiki-jujutsu systems can give a person a false sense of security when technical knowledge is amassed without the necessary attributes to bring it all together. Sparring would alert people to this by revealing their weaknesses, but the nature of submissions on the body's smaller joints doesn't lend itself as well to sparring. Chokes and armbars can be resisted, and there is a short but definite time when the person defending feels the transition from a good defense to a good time to tap.

Take a cross-body armlock, as a typical example. The attacker is already in perpendicular position to his opponent; he's just trying to wrench the arm free from the defender, who's grabbing his own forearm to block the submission. The attacker kicks the hand grabbing the forearm away; the defender's arm unfurls and is quickly extended into lockout. The arc the defender's arm travels from curled defense to extended submission takes a certain amount of time, let's say for hypothetical purposes, one second on a limb this large.

Then you take a wrist, with a very small range of motion, and only a fraction of a second is required to travel the arc from defense to injury. There simply isn't enough time to properly assess when control has been lost and it would be prudent to tap. Either you go with it and take the appropriate ukemi, resist and succeed in retaining control of your balance, or resist and get a broken wrist. The nature of the technique dictates the method of practice, and unfortunately, I don't see how classical jujutsu can be practiced in the dojo with the intensity it was intended for in self-defense situations.

But because you can be very physical, put up maximal resistance, and wait to tap until you have ABSOLUTELY no choice in BJJ, loss in a sparring match is very definite and real. There is a profound impact on the psyche when you know and feel that despite trying your absolute best to survive, you are being massacred. You tap out, smile, shake hands and start again. The person who just dominated you doesn't let it feed their ego, as they have been in your position many times before, and still finds themselves there when dealing with higher ranks and more skilled practitioners. The model of humility is there in front of you to emulate.

Martial arts should promote humility, although ego is often bred through the confidence of mastering physical techniques within a martial art. Humility is then handed to you after a practitioner realizes there are beings of greater skill and mastery in their discipline, yet many of them are devoid of the arrogance often found in the inexperienced. It's hard to have a huge ego when the person who just trounced you has been around the block a few times and realizes his own place in the scheme of things.

So whenever I see a person with an ego out of control in the world of martial arts, I just know he hasn't been lucky enough to have the opportunity of losing with any kind of regularity or consistency. I've lost so many times I couldn't possibly take it personally, or I'd have difficulty justifying my own existence.

After all, it's nothing personal. It's just training.

THE RELIGIOUS EXPERIENCE OF THE UFC

I was still going to high school in Canada when my friend Aaron casually mentioned that there was going to be some kind of fighting event on pay-per-view. I asked what kind of fighting would be in this competition, and he told me, "Every kind. It's going to be karate vs. tae kwon do, judo vs. savate, jiu jitsu vs. something. It's going to be everything vs. everything."

The first thing out of my mouth was, "Are they going to have aikido in there?"

"I don't think so," he said, "I looked, but I didn't see anything."

I thought Aaron was going to record it. I remember him saying he was going to record it, but when I asked how the show was the next Monday at school, he said he didn't know. This was not what I wanted to hear.

"What do you mean you don't know? Weren't you supposed to record it?"

"Yeah, but I didn't have any money."

I was a disappointed, but not terribly distraught since I didn't know exactly what I was missing out on. I did hear what happened, though. Aaron and I were at the gym and one of the regulars there had seen it. He explained how it worked: it was a tournament; you had to fight twice to get to the finals, and it had been a pretty good show. I asked him who won, and he said,

"This little guy from Brazil. He did jiu jitsu. He was really sneaky, you know. Someone would try to punch him, he'd duck and get behind and choke 'em, or put them in some kind of joint-lock."

That's pretty smart, I thought to myself. "Do you remember his name?"

He thought about it for a minute, "It was, uh, it was something like... Man, I thought I had it there. Sorry. I guess I can't remember what it was."

Other guys in the gym were listening to the conversation, and they piped in their opinions. "Hey, you know who I really want to see in there? Chuck Norris. Yah, either that or Steven Seagal. I'd love to see those guys kick ass."

That was the consensus. They wanted to see some of the movie stars get in there and mix it up. Not to see if they could really do it, that thought didn't even enter into the picture. These guys wanted to see the moves done in movies actually executed at full speed, with full contact. Now that's entertainment!

Somebody's recollection of a fight is a poor substitute to actually seeing it, so I was pleased to see ads come up for another tournament a few months later. And this time, I wasn't going to take any chances with Aaron being low on funds. Therefore, I went through the necessary rigmarole of going to the cable company, getting a pay-per-view box, slapping down the deposit, setting it up, and having my two friends over for the fights. Such things cannot be subject to chance.

I was really curious what it was going to be like. I'll admit, I thought it would be a lot like the movies. Spinning, jumping, flying high kicks, an occasional throw, maybe a little stuff on the ground before they scrambled back up to their feet to punch and kick again. But I wasn't expecting what I saw.

Admittedly, UFC II is the most brutal of them all, but also the most illuminating to the classical martial artist. Inoki Ichihara, an incredible karate practitioner from Japan, was easily taken out of his element by Royce Gracie, that "sneaky" Brazilian, and choked into submission. Pat Smith took on Scott Morris, a ninjitsu stylist, and elbowed him into both semi-consciousness and reconstructive surgery. And Johnny Rhodes fought Fred Ettish, in an infamous bout that I remember as the epitome of a martial artist meeting a street fighter.

As I watched, my heart actually went out to Fred. Here he was, a small, wiry guy, probably pretty strong for his size, walking into a mixed martial arts competition with a traditional karate mentality. Even though he stated that he had ultimate faith in both his style and his sensei, I don't really think he understood that this was an entirely different game, that this was not sparring as he knew it.

When he squared off against Johnny Rhodes, he assumed an orthodox karate posture, and fired a crisp front snap kick far away from his target. Basically, all it took was one good overhand right from Johnny, and

Fred Ettish fell to the ground, a gash above his eye, not knowing what to do, but realizing that he was losing very badly. His heart allowed him to hang on, and consequently, he took a beating. If he were to ever make a comeback, I'd definitely be rooting for him.

By the end of the show, it had all been laid out in front of us. Royce Gracie (people were starting to remember his name at this point), had easily rolled through another tournament. The wind had been knocked out of the sails of the classical camp, and illusions of stylistic invincibility were gone. Well, except for maybe Gracie Jiu-Jitsu.

In its place, a new sport was born. Sure, it was a little rough around the edges, not terribly graceful, and it shamelessly played up the possibility of catastrophic injuries through the "no rules" slant (which it would later regret). But at least it had begun with a bang.

I'd never really liked sports before. Whether they were individual or team, it didn't matter. My parents never pushed it and since it was up to me, I didn't get involved in traditional youth activities (football, baseball, basketball, and particularly hockey in Alaska) because I didn't have any interest.

I tried a few things in high school, but it all seemed kind of pointless. If you devoted your life to getting ahead in competitive athletics, you might win a scholarship to a college where you could continue to compete. Then, if you were in an elite minority, you could turn pro after school. That is, if there were professional organizations in your particular sport. If you were a wrestler, you could go to the Olympics, but then what? Coach? Same thing for cross-country skiing, gymnastics, diving, whatever. It just didn't click with me. Why would I want to play football when I, most likely, wouldn't ever play again after high school? I wanted something that could serve me in the long run.

Then martial arts came into the picture. They were a sport, a discipline, an art, and a means of social interaction that I could continue for the rest of my life. Plus, let's not forget, I'd learn martial skill.

But they didn't have trading cards, pennant races, huge stadiums packed with fans, national news coverage, or multi-million dollar contracts for their stars. Being an action hero is the closest you can come to that kind of payoff, and that's different from being a pure martial artist.

I never followed football, baseball, or hockey. I thought they were boring. I probably would have enjoyed, or at least appreciated those sports, had I played. But this was something I did play, something that I could follow, something I could lose myself in by merely watching.

Maybe there's something that I missed along the way. Whether it's simple idolatry, a vicarious extension past your athletic limits, or just a way for a boy to dream, I think following your favorite sport is important. Although Noam Chomsky may analyze it down to a big distraction for the masses, keeping our attention diverted from things that really affect our lives, like political policies, I still think it's important. It adds a little drama to our day; it may inspire us, or inform us of the struggles and triumphs of others on a stage for all to see. At the very least, it gives us a little extra impetus to roll out of bed in the morning because we have something to look forward to.

So finally, after years of watching major sporting events apathetically, I realized what the magic of sports was all about through the UFC. Finally, a sport that I practiced, understood, and personally identified with had come into existence, and I was hooked. It took everything: boxing, kickboxing, judo, jiu-jitsu, karate, tae kwon do, wrestling, and whatever else you want to throw into the mix; combined it, and allowed me to witness with my own eyes answers to martial questions I had been struggling with for years. All done in a format that, to me at least, was undeniably real.

For others however, it's not quite as convincing. I'm not talking about the close-minded conservatives who think it's human cockfighting and are determined to ban it. I'm talking about our own brothers in the martial arts community! They refuse to listen to the Word, to the Truth, to the Light of the UFC. I find it difficult to believe that they would rather close their eyes and damn themselves than be born again under a new baptism.

There's not much I can do other than shake my head. You can try to spread the Word, but you have to be very tactful because, by and large, people don't want to hear it. They get very defensive very quickly if they feel you're insinuating that their art is ineffective.

I should know. I did, and I still do from time to time when people tell me the arts I've studied don't work.

Judo, jujutsu, aikido, iaido, Brazilian Jiu-Jitsu; all have come under attack at one time or another by other martial artists. I take it all in stride, and try to see their points from their perspective.

Others don't. They wear blinders or simply write off what they see. When I was taking tae kwon do, our assistant instructor was a freshly minted black belt, which in his mind, translated into sheer invincibility. Not a physical specimen, mind you. Chubby, 19 or 20 years old, but he had these very flexible hips that allowed him to throw kicks in amazing directions. He was good at tae kwon do, but not awe inspiring. When I asked him about the UFC, he immediately revealed his deeply rooted misunderstanding of the reality of combat.

"The UFC? Yah, I've seen that. Those guys, ahh, they're not really good. I've seen them. They're really slow, and some of the guys are pretty sloppy. If someone tried to shoot in on me, I'd kick their head off."

I'd like to hear him say that while Ken Shamrock or Royce Gracie are in the room, but talk is cheap. Lots of people talk, lots of people talk about fighting, lots of people talk about fighting in the UFC. Few actually do it. Anyone who has the guts to walk through that crowd, step into the octagon, and throw down with everything he's got has earned my respect, even if he loses terribly. It takes courage, and to actually be selected to compete (the caliber of fighters chosen has risen dramatically over the past few years), speaks volumes for a fighter's physical prowess, dedication, and mental toughness to endure the training necessary to become a world-class mixed martial arts fighter.

You have to be able to put your ego aside and overcome your weaknesses, which usually entails some degree of starting over. If you're a great grappler, and can't humble yourself into seeking out a boxing coach and take a few shots learning to survive on your feet, you won't survive in the UFC. It's the same for a lot of strikers who need to learn grappling. You have to be able to become that empty cup that many martial artists wax on about, but haven't actually checked for awhile. It's survival of the fittest, plain and simple.

Which is why I think a lot of people simply ignore the UFC. Maybe it will just go away and they can go back to teaching tae kwon do (or whatever) in isolation, without having to have this constant visual reminder that not only have traditional arts failed to do well, but so have one-dimensional fighters. Who really wants to be reminded that an art they've labored in for years, and which has enriched their lives immeasurably, does very poorly against a skilled opponent?

It's a tough one to swallow, I'll admit, particularly if you're an instructor and teaching that art is your livelihood. But, that's the evolution of things, and I believe cross-training is where it's at. On the flip side, since the instructor would already have a strong suit, it's pretty easy to add to his knowledge, since fighting technology has never been more readily available or easily accessible.

Think about it. Fifty years ago, if you knew any martial art, and went against Joe Schmoe in an alley, chances are you would have done really well. Why? Because Joe had probably had never seen anything other than boxing and wrestling before you threw that Thai kick, tossed him with a tai otoshi, or put that wrist-lock on. Taking someone by surprise through an unorthodox approach gives you a tremendous advantage.

But today? Just look in the phone book, and you can study tae kwon do, karate, kung fu, judo, jujutsu, aikido, sambo, pa kua, tai chi, boxing, kickboxing, silat, or a dozen different arts from all corners of the globe. Since the advent of the VCR, and through modern telecommunications systems such as the Internet and satellite TV, you don't even have to live in a town with martial arts instructors to receive exposure to the latest fighting technology. Watch the UFC on a satellite dish, order a bunch of exotic martial arts videos through a magazine or the Internet, and a wealth of information will be beamed or delivered right to your door.

Ten years ago, grappling was massively underestimated by most martial artists. But today, most practitioners will now acknowledge the importance of grappling, largely because the fighting technology held by the Gracie family has been given public exposure through vale tudo style events.

The Gracies could have continued to convert people slowly to the effectiveness of their system; student by student, through challenge matches and Gracie in Action videotapes. Even then, some people would find it difficult to completely change their beliefs because the general consensus of the martial arts community remained the same: one punch or one kick and you're dead.

By organizing and demonstrating the effectiveness of Gracie Jiu-Jitsu in the UFC, it forced a paradigm shift in the martial arts community at large. People being people, once the majority had acknowledged the effectiveness of grappling, a huge new market was opened with high demand, and the Gracies were there to fill it. But the technology they innovated and refined was out of their hands at that point. People saw, people studied, and people trained. Now it's only a matter of time before the rest of the world catches up. It may take generations, but I believe it will happen.

So the cat is out of the bag, and now that it's free, nobody knows where it's going. It shot out like a bullet and never stopped to look back, just like the fighters who are adopting these techniques and expanding their horizons. In the few years the UFC has been around, the quality of the fighters has risen exponentially, and everybody's learned the game. Boxing combinations, Thai kicks, double-leg takedowns, the guard, armbars, knee bars, chokes, shoulder locks, ankle locks, heel hooks, defensive footwork and octagon tactics are not simply known by an elite minority; almost every fighter entering the UFC is either highly skilled in, or at the very least familiar with, execution of all those techniques.

It's exciting, isn't it? Both martial arts and martial consciousness are evolving at a rate never before seen, thanks to the empirical testing ground the UFC has provided. But, I must admit, the UFC is not the be all and end all of fighting. Actually, despite the fact that they're really fighting, the UFC can be terribly unrealistic.

Let's start with clothes. Most competitors in the UFC don't wear anything more than a pair of shorts and gloves. I've observed that society prefers clothed individuals, and the kind of clothes you're wearing can make a large difference in a fight.

Things would be a lot different if everyone were forced to wear a gi. Not only would judo and jiu jitsu players do a lot better because many of the techniques in their arsenal are gi dependent, but they're also highly skilled at limiting an opponent's mobility solely through how they grasp their clothing. Without clothing, watching two evenly matched opponents grapple can be like watching snakes: slipping, sliding, constantly reversing techniques and positions. With clothes, things are much slower, the friction is greater, and if your opponent knows how to effectively manipulate you through what you're wearing, you can feel pretty helpless. I know. I've been there many times.

Don't forget about footwear. A lot of those foot and leg locks are much harder for opponents to wiggle out of if they're wearing shoes. But that risk would be offset by the huge power increase generated for kicking by a pair of steel-toed boots. Can you imagine a savate champion in the UFC with a pair of cowboy boots? He may not win, but it could be a Phyrric victory for his opponent if he managed to get some shots in.

Next, let's have the fighters begin standing face to face, with no more than a foot between them. That's how a lot of fights start in a bar, with no Big John McCarthy asking them if they're ready before they "get it on." Or, if that still seems too even, flip a coin, and have the loser of the toss stand with his back to his opponent, so he can get jumped. You know, add that element of surprise.

I could go on and on with other ways the UFC could change its format to more closely approximate the conditions of a street fight. Friends, weapons, alcohol, light conditions, even the surface you're on would change the tactics you adopt. I think you'd agree that the UFC would be much different if everyone were required to wear a T-shirt, denim jacket, a pair of jeans and steel-toed boots, then squared off in an asphalt octagon.

But it's not like that, which in a way, gives it a kind of nobility. It's purified combat, taking place in an environment where advantages are evened and variables minimized. It allows technique, strategy, and athleticism to shine, maximizing the safety of the competitors while still demanding them to give it their all. It is a highly controlled arena, but within the wide parameters of combat that have been established in the UFC and MMA competition, a tremendous amount of martial freedom and technical creativity is allowed.

Some martial artists I know criticize the rules established by the UFC. No biting, no eye gouging, no fish-hooking, no small joint manipulation, no pressure points, and a few others. Let's go over some of these rules.

Biting, as Mike Tyson has shown us, is a savage act that may inflict permanent damage, but will not, by itself, incapacitate an opponent.

No fish-hooking is a good one, because if somebody sticks their finger in their opponent's mouth, they're asking to get bitten, so it goes hand in hand with the no-biting rule.

Eye gouging may incapacitate some, but if they're still ticking after you've done it, all you've really done is anger them to the point where now they're going to kill you.

No small joint manipulation is intended to keep people from breaking fingers and toes. But fighters are tough, and they're able to eat that pain, especially if they have a more substantial submission nearly in place.

Overall, by entering the UFC and adhering to the rules of the sport, you're not really giving up all that much, but some people still insist that they're so unfairly hampered by the restrictions that they can't really show what their arts are capable of.

My take on it is this. Yes, these can be effective techniques for primal defense, but if you don't have the ability to fight without your beloved eye gouge or the freedom to bite, you're simply deficient in martial ability. The UFC is a method of testing martial prowess, and if you don't want to test yourself because you believe the conditions are unfair, then when will you test yourself? When you get jumped in the street?

If that's the only time you elect to spar, you're not going to do very well, because you haven't developed the attributes or timing necessary to activate your techniques or the ability to stay calm in high-pressure situations. Don't depend on the dirty stuff, thinking it will all be over when you jab him in the eye. You may get lucky, but I wouldn't count on it, especially with vital areas and pressure points. Pressure points work, but not under all conditions, and some people are insensitive to them. You've got to have a backup.

The rules may be limiting, but it's a limited skill set that will really come back to haunt you in permanently impairing somebody's vision or biting a chunk out of a leg. Haven't you ever lost your temper? Haven't you ever made a mistake? Putting somebody in an immobilization or submission technique will allow time for both of you to calm down, and act as a buffer before actions are committed that may corner you into a lifetime of regret. Plus, isn't it more admirable to be able to effectively control or subdue an attacker while injuring him as little as possible?

I think so. After all, the only time a lot of people actually get to use their martial training is holding down a drunken friend. You don't want to hurt him, you just need him to calm down. That's real skill and compassion, and it's real life.

The UFC is beyond hobby martial artists. It's the bigtime, it's going to "the show." Most people are not born with the genetics of Mark Kerr, have access to the mentorship and experience of Carlson Gracie, or have the ability to devote themselves to full-time training as they do at the Lion's Den. The ranks of professional fighters are growing, and because of the severity of their training, they are distancing themselves from your average martial arts practitioner. But that's okay, it's just the evolution of things.

The modern era has provided us access to the best hand to hand combat techniques from every corner of the globe, refined over centuries of experimentation. Couple this with advances in sports physiology and scientific training methods, and it should be no surprise that these fighters are the greatest martial athletes the world has ever known. Weight training, whey protein, nutritional analysis, anabolic steroids, supplementation, PNF stretching, visualization, biofeedback, target heart rates; all of these have propelled the modern athlete to push the envelope of human capability.

Which is why I don't buy it when your average martial artist starts ragging on the realism of the UFC simply because they don't allow a few select actions. Even worse are those that dismiss the fighters offhand because- well, I'll put it in their words:

"Yeah, I think my sensei could take on Mark Coleman or Rickson Gracie."

I couldn't believe my ears. "Are you serious? You really think he could beat them?"

"Of course. Those guys train for competition, and competitions have rules. They don't train for combat. So they're going to be limited in a real fight."

Sometimes, I fear these people cannot be helped. Maybe they forget that their ace in the hole, the dirty stuff, can also be used by their opponent who's developed his attributes, put in his time sparring, and knows how to be consistently and overwhelmingly aggressive. UFC fighters may not know weapon defenses, or tactics for multiple assailants, but I'll put my money on almost any of them over a local bar tough if it's simply fisticuffs. As an uninitiated observer of the UFC once noted, "Wow, the toughest guy on your block loses in 20 seconds..."

That's the reality of it, and I think that's one of the reasons why it excites me so much. There's unpredictability in a fight, and the skill level these competitors operate at turns the martial into art. It's breathtaking to watch two martial athletes at the top of their games square off in a contest that exemplifies the crux of the human condition. Skill, strategy, discipline, honor, respect, passion and pain intertwine momentarily in an expression of total energy and emotion. It is all beauty, it is all passion, it is all heart.

It hits me at a very deep, almost primal level. My heart races, appetite disappears, and pupils dilate. The UFC is my drug of choice. If they had it on as often as football or baseball, I don't think I'd ever leave the house.

How strong is this addiction? If I had to choose between watching a UFC in person, or going on a date with a stunning Playboy Playmate... I'd have to take the UFC. Yes, I know many readers out there are booing me right now, but also know for a fact that there are some who understand. They'd do the same thing, 'cause they're just as sick as me.

Choosing between a live broadcast of the UFC and going out with a Playboy Playmate would be different. It depends on who's fighting. If it wasn't a very strong card, I'd probably record it and go out with the girl.

But I'm trying to cut down on my Playmate consumption these days, so chances are, I'd be watching the UFC... alone.

Religion must have seized people this way in the past, inspiring a kind of impassioned devotion. Once the UFC is on, I admit, I'm no longer in control. Something else takes over. Some might say I'm in rapture. Tempt me with women, poke me with pins, I am wholly unaffected by my gaze upon the light.

Sometimes, I can't even control my body. I couldn't sit still during the famous Oleg Taktarov/Tank Abbot final of UFC 6, so I nervously paced in front of the television, arms folded across my chest, one hand on my chin. After Oleg finally won, I quietly pondered if God was keeping tabs on all of these UFC debts. I hope not. The afterlife won't be pretty if these promises actually count.

Whether it's the modern continuation of the combative traditions, or the infectious passion of an emerging sport, I feel that the UFC has a lot to offer, not just to martial artists, but to everyone with an open mind. It is a microcosm, playing upon one of the most fundamental dilemmas in our existence: the tension of facing another person in one-on-one opposition. Yet that very confrontation has the power to enlighten us, since nothing makes you feel more alive than imminent conflict or an unavoidable fight. Our evolution and assimilation into the information age has not been without repercussions, so the UFC is simply reclaiming a vital part of our past, celebrating the human experience in greater totality.

It may not be me fighting out there in the octagon, but in a way, it is. I'm right there, every time, taking notes and inspiration from the competitors. I feel I've learned a lot, and realize that far beyond the biomechanics of executing techniques lie much deeper truths: Preparation is everything; there are many ways to win a fight; class is more endearing than victory; and a loss may cause a man to leave, but the fighter still remains. These are lessons for us all, I think, and I look forward to learning more of them in the years to come, as I watch the UFC alone, in a Playmateless existence, quietly hoping God's lost track of my promises...

THE UNINVITED VISITOR

Sensei was out of town, and I had just finished teaching the Wednesday night class when a blond guy in his early twenties strolled into the dojo. Immediately I bowed off the mat, made a beeline to him, and shook his left hand. I had to head him off at the pass because it was clear that this individual was a little "altered," if you know what I mean.

Barefoot in jeans and a woolen pullover (not to mention the green boomerang sticking out the back of his collar), he was a bit dirty, and very wide-eyed.

I asked if I could help him and answer any questions he might have. He asked a few coherent things before going off about how he loved the dojo and how he'd like his house in Japan to look just like it. He also thought that it was refreshing to see how clean the walls were, because as he explained, when the Japanese came to this country, "they took their ninja swords and covered the walls of their dojos with the blood of Americans." This, of course, was before he revealed that he had been buried in ink up to his chest for the past seven lifetimes. He dug me, loved my explanations, and I shook his right hand before amicably parting. Out the door, he headed into the night. What can you say? It was good acid.

He was relatively harmless, but hanging around a dojo, you get an opportunity to see a variety of people come in and out, some invited, some not. Monterey is a pretty nice area, so there aren't a lot of thugs coming in off the street, trying to test their stuff. But it does happen.

Once a huge man stumbled in after class, drunk from the bar next door, and asked Sensei if he thought he could flip him around like he saw the students being thrown. He was about six feet tall, and at least two hundred and fifty pounds, so it certainly would have been a challenge to get this guy airborne. I didn't catch what Sensei said to him at first, but the guy was kind of puzzled by what he had heard, and changed his question to "So if I went one (left jab)/two (right cross slowly demonstrated toward Sensei's head), you still think you can do it?"

Sensei's reply shocked him even more than the first. "You don't understand. There would be no one/two. There would be only one, and it would be over. There wouldn't even be a two."

"You really think so?"

"I don't think so, I know so. There are people who look like they can really do things, and there are people who can really do things. I am one of the people who can."

Sensei said it with such assurance that you could see it take the fight out our large friend, and finally, seeking confirmation on the secret of Sensei's confidence, he asked, "You use angles, don't you?"

"Yes," Sensei answered, "you are very intelligent. We use angles and leverage." And with that, they shook hands and the drunken challenger headed out the door.

That's one way to handle challenges, taking the fight out of a person through psychological or situational manipulation. This, I believe, is a large part of aiki-jujutsu as I've come to find out, which was different from my original view.

After putting on a children's martial arts camp, Sensei, Sheila, and I were on a long drive back to Monterey when I asked him for his explanation of the difference between jujutsu and aiki jujutsu. Was it simply that aiki jujutsu used an opponent's momentum more efficiently than jujutsu, and depended on that commitment to a larger degree as an integral part of the technique? He said that was partially correct, but there was more to it than that. It took me a while to digest what he said, but I think I've got it now.

Psychological distractions, fake-outs, knockout blows through pressure points, switching an attacker's target to track your hand instead of your face; all of these are tricks and strategies of aiki jujutsu. But do they work? Well. . . yes and no.

"The more aiki jujutsu something is, the more bullshit it is," Sensei explained, "which doesn't mean it doesn't work, it just means you have to set up the right situation for it to happen."

Then he went on about knockout blows. Occasionally, he'll knock out a trusted student at the dojo for a demonstration, but he warned me that if someone is tense or expecting a blow to come, it's not going to work. You have to create the circumstance, maybe talk to them, calm them down, cajole them, then when the timing's right, deliver the strike unexpectedly.

It's really no different than boxing, wrestling, judo, jiu jitsu, or any other sport. Your competition knows what you're up to and is generally familiar with the attacks in your arsenal. You have to use combinations of techniques to set your opponent up, or nothing's going to work for you. To throw an experienced judo player in a tournament without some kind of feint or set-up is nearly impossible. These things don't just happen; they must be made to happen.

Which is one reason why you don't learn many of the tricks of aiki jujutsu before the upper levels of Seibukan. Strategies using real-world variables can fail, and you better have a strong base of concrete physical skills to serve as a backup plan. But it's good to know that there are more strategies and options available to a person than they might initially imagine. In the movie Pumping Iron, Arnold Schwarzenegger explained how he could talk opponents into losing before ever stepping foot on the stage of Mr. Olympia, and advocated using methods outside the arena of competition to sway fortune your way. Life is full of variables, why not be creative and use them in your favor?

So what do you when a drunken challenger walks in the dojo and wants to prove how tough he is or how "real" the training isn't? I don't know. Some people field challenges, some invite them to join the class and feel the training for themselves; others get a large student to act as an escort, guiding them to their next stop. It's a recurring problem that will never go away, so new solutions must be constantly sought. One instructor I knew had the answer for his school. If someone came to issue a challenge, he'd walk to the back of the dojo, get his pistol, calmly show it to them, and ask, "Alright, just how real do you want to get?"

Good question. Do you just want to disprove a particular technique or make it open hand-to-hand combat? Are the challengers aware that the instructor they chose may intend to use weapons, or feel that anything goes, including bites, groin shots, and eye-gouges? A challenge means a tap out to some and a life-or-death struggle to others. Most people don't want to acknowledge that kind of gravity, but a primal response to what a person perceives to be a life-or-death situation is a reality. I don't think anybody would want to really push the envelope on the question of how real they'd like to get because so few could stomach the truth.

A good friend of mine from Indonesia brought it all into focus as we drove to Santa Cruz to train at Claudio's. We were jabbering away about different styles, combat effectiveness, the truth in martial arts; in other words, the usual topics for two martial addicts. Then he blew me away by saying, "You know, it's all bullshit anyway. It doesn't matter if you know Brazilian Jiu-Jitsu or JKD concepts. In my country, if you speak out against the government, you'll be floating face down in a river the next day, and it doesn't matter how much you know, there's nothing you can do to stop it."

That is far more real than I'd ever like to get. Makes the drunk guy throwing out a challenge seem pretty inconsequential, and an overall waste of time. It puts things in perspective, for me at least. It may be tempting to showcase your skills on the street, but consider this: After the fight is over, can the barely victorious really be considered "the winner"? Does the thrill of victory last longer than its legal ramifications, or the healing time of a fractured hand? Think about it.

We're all role-playing in martial arts, taking our turns in the game, so when challenges arise, I think it's best to handle them peacefully and continue on. If you select otherwise, be sure to pick your fights carefully, since the one you choose could be your last.

FIGHTERS, PHILOSOPHERS, AND ATHLETES

Coming from a background in classical martial arts, I found it hard to reconcile the skill disparities in martial artists, their arts, and their ranks in those respective arts.

Initially, I thought that if you had a black belt in any art, you were basically lethal. A person with a black belt was not somebody you wanted to mess with.

If they knew karate, it was a "one punch, one kill" type of situation. A tae kwon do stylist could beat you down using only their feet, and an aikido practitioner would break your wrist into a hundred shards. The ancient knowledge and anatomical secrets that had been passed on to the chosen few were enough to strike fear in the heart of me. I was just thankful their code of ethics restrained them in exercising those powers.

But as I spent time training, I was disappointed to realize my pre-conceived notions were far off. For the longest time I tried to force the experiential data I had gathered into a paradigm of what I believed martial arts should be, instead of what they actually were. Only near the end of my apprenticeship commitment did I toss it all out and come up with a new model that I believe is more accurate- though certainly not definitive.

I'm a martial artist. Identifying myself as such, the integrity of what a martial artist is couldn't be compromised in my mind, yet I saw things everywhere that didn't add up.

It was difficult to make sense of it all. Beginners don't have the kind of perspective and experience that many martial veterans take for granted. So they "buy" into an art, investing themselves physically in training, intellectually in theory, and emotionally in their loyalty to their chosen art, often coming to its defense with a terse dismissal of criticism.

It's only natural this would happen, but later on, if they end up studying another art, then a reconciliation must take place. Tae kwon do and jujutsu can't both be the "ultimate" art, just as aikido, silat, judo, karate, shootfighting, and others fail to be "the best." Some are better than others, depending on what you're looking for, and some may not be for you. Diversity is a good thing.

Before I actually trained, the more esoteric martial arts held the most appeal to me. I liked the idea of secret knowledge. I wanted some of that. Then after I trained a few years, I realized that knowledge is not enough. True effectiveness relies heavily on both techniques and the training methods. Some systems have more subtle and varied techniques than others do, without the pressure of live and resistant situations. Others take a more physical, sport oriented approach, through conditioning, repetitive drills, and sparring.

A common question posed to me regarding martial arts would come from casual observers and friends. They'd watch a class, or catch the tail end of a training session waiting for me. Then they'd ask a variation of this fundamental question:

"So Roy, tell me something. That thin little guy in the class, the one that weighed a buck twenty five. He's a higher rank than you are? He is? So if you guys got in a fight, he'd kick your ass? You know, in a street fight or say you're in a bar... if you guys got into it, he'd be able to do that thing you guys practice (insert chopping motions here). He wouldn't? Then why is he a higher rank? Doesn't that mean he's better than you?"

It's a fair question. It was tough for me to answer without going into a long tirade, and most people aren't looking for a defensive justification of an art via technical proficiency vs. real life effectiveness. All they want to know is, "Can he kick ass?"

Once I stepped away, removed myself from stylistic biases and was really honest with myself, I had to admit it. Most martial artists I've come across in my life cannot kick ass, and are delusional about their abilities.

Don't get me wrong. There are absolute killers out there in the world of martial arts, guys you should never mess with under any circumstances, guys that would end the fight before you even knew what happened. But that's not most people. That's the tough minority.

Many martial artists don't realize there are people off the street with no refined technical skill, have never stepped foot in a dojo, but will out muscle and overwhelm you with such fury that you won't even know which way is up.

Unless your technique is really good, and your body has been trained to respond to that kind of intensity, then their speed, strength, and savagery will win. Shoot a little adrenaline in a person's system and you'll be amazed at how an untrained, ordinary Joe becomes a wild nightmare of toughness and fear.

So how can people receive a black belt and not able to defend themselves against an angry construction worker? This was another philosophical quandary, as I tried to have it make sense without concluding that martial arts were bullshit, because I knew they weren't. They just weren't consistent. I mulled over some of the inconsistencies I'd seen.

What do you do with the elderly gentleman who generously devotes time to an art, is knowledgeable about it history, knows all the requirements for black belt, but has difficulty with the physical execution because his body is a wreck? Does he deserve a black belt?

What about the young wrestler who, on the street, could decimate everyone in the dojo, but is stuck as a green belt? What should his rank be?

What do you do with the guy who knows a little karate and lot of karazy, and would prevail on heart, intensity, and fury? Isn't it about who's the best fighter?

I thought it was, but experience has forced me to categorize martial arts participants in a different way than I would've originally believed. Under the blanket label of "martial artists," I have sub-sectioned them into three divisions: fighters, philosophers, and athletes.

Fighters are primarily concerned with what works, regardless of how it looks. Stylistic considerations are not a concern. Rank is not as much of an issue with this group. The need for a well-rounded martial education is of utmost importance in order to prepare them for whatever may come their way. Applicable street tactics are always in the back of their minds. Weapons defenses, ground fighting, standup skills, control and arrest techniques- all are valued and practiced with equal fervor. Unfortunately, during exercises of lower practical value or a more esoteric nature, they often feel they're wasting time. Many are not shy in voicing complaints. They often bring up "What if..." scenarios, or ask direct questions to the teacher during demonstrations, where others would wait. The desire to turn up the intensity during class, occasionally to an unexpected or inappropriate level, can give them a reputation for being rough or uncooperative. Many times they test out the techniques in real life conditions (a.k.a. bar fight), and feel good about it, since they feel that everything they're learning is supposed to be used if the opportunity exists.

Philosophers are looking for the beauty of the martial movements and the integration of philosophy into daily life. The martial art is the vehicle for this moral refinement. Rank can sometimes be an issue, as philosophers can sometimes get ahead of themselves in the knowledge vs. skill debate. In giving constructive criticism to lower ranks, they're able to delve far deeper than body mechanics, and encourage the student to monitor subtle arenas such as intent and presence. They may identify very strongly with the ethical code of warriors past. Meditation is valued. Cultivation of internal energy is desired. They would rather wait with a question and ask after class than put the instructor in a potentially embarrassing situation. The history, tradition, and lore of their particular martial discipline is studied and cherished. Martial arts are seen as occupying a higher function than merely sport or exercise. Aesthetics are observed with great sensitivity in many areas: dojo and uniform appearance, cleanliness, etiquette, adherence to foreign terms and traditions, et cetera. Devoted and knowledgeable, they are often excellent ambassadors of an art.

Athletes enjoy the rigors of competition and celebrate the improvement it creates. Attribute development for speed, power, endurance, flexibility and aggressiveness is encouraged and applauded. Athletes would rather test their techniques on the mat than on the street, and often have a strong bond with their team members. Strategy and innovation are appreciated, as they can give a competitor the upper hand through unpredictability and surprise within the confines of the rules governing their sport. Some athletes may not look on their discipline as being anything more than a workout, and a training session without sparring is incomplete. Athletes like to do, rather than talk about doing, or analyze the spiritual ramifications of doing. They like to sweat, and can expend tremendous amounts of energy. Because of the intensity of their training, they can eat pain and bear discomfort well. They love "the game," and are concerned with what works for them in that game. The drilling of basics makes them lightning quick. If a beginner were to step into their arena, they'd feel helpless against a seasoned competitor. This difference in skill makes it all seem effortless.

A well-rounded martial artist, in the fullest sense of the word, should be a strong combination of fighter, philosopher, and athlete. Everyone is a combination of these categories, and usually weighted in a particular direction. Long-term training and exposure to a variety of participants will tend to even practitioners out, but unless they're aware that they need to become more athletic, more streetwise, or see the bigger picture of their art's function in society, they will remain imbalanced.

Athletes are probably the safest group in remaining imbalanced. All their physical development pays heavy dividends in a street fight or crisis situation, as they can often overwhelm their opponents with deftly applied power, ending the fight before it really begins. That's why it's my belief is that you must be a martial athlete to fully develop into a martial artist. Once you have the attributes, you can manufacture yourself into a formidable mix of fighter and philosopher, since the raw materials are already at your disposal.

Philosophers are probably the most difficult to convince that they need to become more well rounded, since many believe the work they're doing is transcendent of violence and competition, leaving them the least safe on the street. The philosopher will project into the nether and leave the body behind, while the transcendence they're looking for is right there in front of them, and must be achieved through the body, not ahead of it.

That's what makes martial arts such a fantastic medium for self-development. It's your body, and you have to take full responsibility for its training and conditioning. You can't delegate it to another body. You can't escape the pain, exhaustion, and effort required on a day-to-day basis. If you are able to eat bitter and dedicate yourself, you'll see improvement and results. It's very simple: you get out what you put in, but there are no shortcuts. You can't intellectualize it away- you have to actually feel it. Some things must be endured.

Fighters may be drawn to martial arts because of the techniques, but it's not really an efficient way for them to learn the bare bones of self-defense. That's why I've found that most of them don't stick around in traditional arts. Those who do stick around are eventually ironed out in those three categories, and become refreshingly open and practical martial artists.

But the dissatisfied fighter who bounces from art to art, picking up techniques here and there, leads us to a fundamental question: What does it really take to protect yourself? Nothing fancy and nothing stylized. Just the necessary tools for bare bones street defense.

A longtime practitioner I know asked one of his private students what he wanted to learn. Did he want to know how to simply win a street fight, or did he want to learn some cool moves he could show to his friends that were also fun to practice? The student wanted a little of both, with which my friend happily complied, but if he'd only wanted street tactics, I asked myself, what would he have taught and how long would it have taken?

I say it could happen with three techniques over three months. A Muay Thai kick, a jab/cross punching combination, and a rear naked choke. I think if those basic techniques were diligently practiced under proper supervision, with real time drills, you'd be better prepared for a street conflict in 3 months than most traditional practitioners after years of practice.

The list of techniques is almost arbitrary, and could just as easily be a sidekick, straight blast, and an outside trip. What really matters is the method of practice, getting it to the point where intelligent, scientific movements are instinctive.

A Japanese martial artist once explained to me that the goal of physical training is perfection, but the definition of perfection must be clearly understood. Westerners tend to think of perfection as an unreachable goal where techniques cannot be performed any better. The Japanese view perfection as an achievable point in training where your body responds without conscious thought.

That made a lot of sense to me. In a crisis situation, you never rise to your level of expectation, but instead sink to your level of training. And when you get the opportunity to meet masters with a lifetime of training, the precise nature of their techniques can approximate "perfection", in the Japanese sense of the word.

On the wall of my old judo dojo was a poster of Mike Swain leaving the mat after winning the world championships. I thought that was the closest I'd ever get to meeting him, but I had to opportunity to not only attend one of his seminars, I was chosen to be Mike's demonstration partner for the day. It was quite an experience. Just having Mike grab my gi was enough to let me know that this was not an ordinary man. There's something special about contact with a high-level martial artist. It's an underlying density to their physique that stems from years and years of consistent training. This could be what students of Morihei Ueshiba described when they said that grabbing his arm was like touching steel wrapped in cotton.

I've had several judo masters toss me before, but none made it feel as effortless as Mike Swain. He was a machine. His body sprang into action perfectly balanced, ready to explode, in the fraction of a second I was off-balanced by him snapping his wrists. His foot sweeps were unbelievable. Impeccable timing and body alignment added up to technique so clean it made me giddy just receiving it. It must be magic, right? No. Some sort of esoteric secret he picked up training with the Japanese?

Actually, it's simple. Speed x technique = power was the formula Mike Swain gave us, and hearing that hit home with me. Being in the right place at the right time, using the momentum of a properly aligned and balanced body in motion is what gives you that illusion of effortlessness, since the strain we recognize as using strength comes from segmented, partially committed attempts at techniques. The gymnastic nature of turning your body into a dynamic weapon through total commitment to a strike or throw takes faith earned through hard training and many repetitions.

But the Big Lie perpetrated in martial arts is that techniques are effortless, instead of simply feeling effortless, and strength isn't necessary to be effective. In fact, nothing could be further from the truth.

Think of a line, with 100 percent strength on the far left, and 100 percent technique on the far right. Both ends of the spectrum are theoretical voids; neither can really exist. Every technique requires strength from the body's musculature, and pure power is an equal impossibility because some degree of angles and leverage must to be employed for one body to affect another. Nevertheless, work with me here...

Strength and technique work hand in hand, and are both necessary in the creation of power, which is what martial arts are all about. That's the most basic aim of martial arts: learning how to cleverly overpower your opponent.

If you're strong enough, there's no need to study martial arts, aside from personal development. The principles of distraction, angles, and leverage are designed to magnify the power of individuals whose physical strength is inferior to that of their opponents. As far as effectiveness goes, it doesn't matter where the power comes from. An equal amount of power can come from a large quantity of brute strength or refined technique, but both are capable of doing the same amount of work.

As martial artists, we are continually adjusting the ratio of strength to technique, aiming to settle in at the technical side of the spectrum. When technique isn't quite right or the angles are a little off, strength can often make up the difference. It is the lubricant of technique, smoothing out the rough spots until your body develops the speed and intuitive feel to exploit opportunities on the path of least resistance.

Ideally, very little strength is used in a properly executed technique, but this is very different from saying strength isn't necessary. I understand, of course, that sometimes stating the position that strength doesn't matter or isn't necessary is necessary to shift a person's perspective. It's a pleasure to tap to technique, and a terrible thing indeed to be mauled into submission, so lofting an ideal of effortlessness is a strategy to get students headed down the road towards clean, technical training. But some get frustrated when the words they hear ("strength doesn't matter") are disproved in physical reality, over and over again.

Perhaps a modification is in order: Strength matters less the better your technique is, but some amount of strength is always required. That strength can also be used in different ways. Sometimes it's required for speed in order to execute a throw, or it's squeezing your body around a limb in order to go for a submission. It doesn't matter. Strength will always be necessary. The need for strength will diminish if you're training properly, but it will never disappear completely.

Aspiring martial artists should be warned that it takes a lot of effort and persistence to develop crisp techniques with sharp timing. It really is paradoxical: you have to be tough and resilient to get to a point where you only have to use a little strength to get the job done.

I wonder if instructors sometimes forget this, because they execute clean techniques ingrained over years of experience. If they happen to find themselves in a situation where a little extra juice is needed, it's easily summoned from reserves, since they've already been through the process.

It isn't strength vs. technique; it's strength working with technique in the creation of power, or the ability to do work. It's all about power, it always has been. Martial arts, business, foreign policy, personal relationships- everything in our lives revolves around power. Power gets things done, but knowledge isn't power. It takes personal will to bring knowledge to power.

Martial knowledge is nothing more than an exercise in physics and physiology. You can know how to do a thousand techniques, but unless you're actually able to perform and apply them in a moment of crisis, all you've acquired will be useless. Knowledge is power only when applied, and the power of martial techniques can only be applied through the process of training. You can only know a technique if you practice it, and you have to practice all the time for true proficiency. Otherwise, forget about it. True power, true effectiveness, only comes through constant application.

This application keeps us grounded and real. Gaining strength anchors you to reality by forcing you to push your limits through muscular exertion, and apply effort to the point of failure. While strength may not be an end in itself, distancing yourself from the dirty hands and daily toil of working out is a dangerous proposition. Building strength serves as a reminder of how much effort it takes to make things happen in this imperfect world.

The "effortless" techniques displayed by masters cannot be shortcut to by a conceptual understanding of an art; it is arrived at over a lifetime of training, shifting the ratio of strength to technique by refining sensitivity, position, and timing. Strive for technique but back it with strength. Hopefully, you'll never need it, but it's good to know it's there. It's a terrible feeling to come up short in any situation, and if your life is dependent on that debt, serious preparation is necessary. Be conservative and keep a little extra in your strength account. That way, you'll never find yourself in the red, with no one to bail you out.

THE ENGLISH PATIENT

Sensei Toribio was out of town again, so Sheila was in charge. After teaching a long series of classes, she was too tired to talk in an indirect manner. So she cut right to the chase.

"Roy, you see that woman sitting in the chair?" We both looked over to the visitors viewing area, where an attractive, dark-haired woman in her early thirties was waiting. "Well, she's going to have to stay here tonight, because if she doesn't, she's going to end up in a park or sleeping outside. And..." she hesitated for second, weighing the conflict between additional information and confidentiality, "and that's all I can tell you right now," she shrugged. There was a hint of exasperation in her voice.

"No problem. I totally understand," I said, then reassured her that I would do everything I could to offer assistance. Obviously, the first thought to enter my mind was that this woman was the victim of domestic violence. It seemed logical that she would seek the sanctuary of a martial arts school, especially one with such a warm, family atmosphere, where she knew she'd be protected. I'd have probably done the same thing had I been in her position.

Francesca seemed nice enough, this pretty woman with an English accent, so whether it was sharing food or lending her clothes, I did whatever I could to offer aid and support. She stayed in the tatami room, which is, in comparison to the loft, the crème de la crème of dojo life.

Perhaps it's not surprising that one night turned into a couple of days, and a couple of days turned into a few weeks. She couldn't go back to England because there was threat of bodily harm revolving around a mysterious lawsuit, and she couldn't work, because she didn't have a green card. It should go without saying that she didn't have any money, so she was just hanging out at the dojo, trying to extend her holiday in America, or whatever it was she was up to.

It only took few days to get wise to her, and I was forthright in expressing my distrust to Sheila. Sheila felt obligated to give her the benefit of the doubt, which I understood, and I urged her to keep her eyes and ears open as well.

Francesca was a true dichotomy. She had a face that made you want to believe, and a mouth that spewed lies you just couldn't. Having seen for myself her utter lack of athletic ability and coordination, I had a hard time buying her tale of surviving an assault by two men in an alley, much less catching the weapon one was wielding in mid-strike with her hands.

To be fair, this was back when she was "working undercover in a Belgian strip club," so I assume her fighting skills were better at that time. Her covert–op training was paying off in her current situation, as she exhibited a mastery of psychological warfare. Francesca headed up a disturbing disinformation campaign; tarring my name with the wickedest tales.

Francesca pulled students aside at the dojo, one by one, and described the unspeakable: I would rise in the dead of night, go out on the deck, and crush snails under my feet. Yes, that's right. Under cover of darkness, I'd work out my daily frustrations on the snails, stomping my weight on their crispy shells. Apparently I enjoyed it.

Several students approached me about this and similar assertions, and I loathed her more and more. Nevertheless, I was told to give her private lessons in order to get her up to speed, so she could join the uchideshi program. If she was going to be living in the dojo, she had to train, and given her current level of coordination, she'd never make it through the regular classes.

I was less than thrilled about this forced interaction. Despite doing my best to remain cordial and offer efficient instruction, I can't deny that the thought of snapping her little wrists like the shell of a snail seemed very appealing. She was putting an earnest effort out there to learn what I was offering, though, and by the end of the lesson, she could approximate the strikes, but still never really got the hang of the rolls. Close enough.

Sensei T. came back into town and was briefed on the situation. Instructing class that night, he had us running through our usual warm-up sequence, including extended rolls. Francesca usually sat out for this portion of the warm-up, but on that particular night, she ran toward the pad everyone had been jumping over, stopped just before hitting it, and looked directly at Sensei T. He immediately told her to do it, and she launched herself into the air, landing perfectly and completely on her skull. Everyone gasped as we watched her literally bounce off her head then stumble to her feet.

That could have been it right there. Not only was that the kind of fall that could have left her paralyzed, but had she been injured, she could have sued the dojo and that could have been the end of Seibukan Jujutsu. I'm certain she hadn't signed any kind of liability release, and I know for a fact that she never paid a dime for her uniform, lessons, or accommodations. Maybe she could have added another lawsuit to her already impressive collection.

Luckily, she was unharmed, and before long, as the vibe in the dojo turned against her, she found her next meal ticket and moved on. She preyed upon one of the nicest guys at the dojo, probably worked her undercover Belgian strip club charms, and accepted his invitation to move in. It was well over a year before I ever saw him again. I never talked to him about

Francesca. I'm sure his memories of her are even more painful than mine.

There's something about a dojo, especially Seibukan dojo, which makes it easy to spot scammers, egos, and the like. I think it's the white mat, clear open spaces, and minimalist design that serves as an easy base for contrast, because unlike the outside world, there aren't a million distractions diminishing your sensitivity. Dirt is hard to see on a sidewalk, but easily spotted in a clean room. Without obstruction in an open dojo, energy is allowed to flow freely, so on a nonverbal, intuitive level, you can feel when someone has a hidden agenda, massive ego, or is just a little bit off. It's subtle, but it's there. You know something's wrong, even if you can't put your finger on it.

Even though the dojo may make it easier to discern the wicked and the weird, that doesn't mean they aren't welcomed or given an opportunity. A dojo will never be a perfect place because it's giving students the benefit of the doubt, allowing all to improve themselves through the discipline of martial arts. If you're there for the wrong reason, just know that it's readily apparent.

If you start with the wrong reason for joining a dojo, but stay with it long enough, you may be surprised at how your original focus will have shifted to something more substantial, and ultimately, more beneficial. Maybe all Francesca needed to do was stick with it and continue training. I'm sure it would have ironed out a few issues, but if she doesn't want to train, then that's fine too. She can do whatever she wants. Just keep her away from me.

INSTRUCTORS, BROTHERS, AND BLACKBELTS

My brother was in trouble, and needed some help.

Rod was five years older than I was and had been living in Las Vegas for the past four years. He moved there with a girlfriend, but after some employment issues and a hard breakup, Rod slipped into a depression. No one in the family knew what to do.

Still living in Alaska, I volunteered to go to Las Vegas and check out the situation. I was prepared to move him if necessary. Where I didn't know, but anywhere else had to be better than where he was at. I flew down and we spent some time together. I met his friends, and came away with the impression that things were on the upswing. But after moving to Monterey, I was informed that his situation had gotten worse.

Sensei and I had a tight relationship, and this was of great concern to me, so I kept him abreast of all the events as they occurred. Finally, I asked him for a favor. Could Rod come to Monterey and also become an uchideshi? If so, everything would work out in my mind. How could you not turn your life around in a dojo full of positive people, with required training to keep you in check?

Sensei agreed to give Rod a chance, and I relayed that message to my brother. It took a month or two for Rod to tie up loose ends and finally leave Las Vegas, but he did it, arriving at the dojo on a Sunday in April.

Carolynn and I were hanging out in the loft when we heard a knock at the front door. Peering through the loft window out front, I spied my brother standing on the sidewalk. He looked very thin. As Sensei would later tell him, "When I saw you for the first time... I saw death."

But this was a new beginning, and after hugging him, I introduced him to Carolynn, unloaded his stuff, and got him settled in. Carolynn and I thought it would be a good idea if we showed him some techniques, to give him an idea of what Seibukan Jujutsu was like. We thought the kihon waza, the basic techniques of the shodan level, would be the most logical place to start.

Carolynn and I dressed out, bowed to each other, and went through all 19 techniques at a moderate pace, while Rod watched from a chair. We bowed again after finishing, looked over at him, and saw an expression that is best described as fear. I think he was expecting a punching and kicking demonstration, and consequently, didn't understand the grabs, pins, rolls and throws he was seeing. No matter, he'd understand soon enough. The next day he was in regular classes, thrown into the mix, doing his best.

Rod hadn't exercised in years. He was stiff and a little uncoordinated at first, but his body gradually awoke and remembered what it was like to be athletic. Rod was a decent basketball player and even competed at the Junior National level in volleyball, but that had been years ago, back in high school.

Sensei met Rod briefly the next day before having to leave town. He may have been going to Japan, I'm not sure, but since he'd be gone for a number of weeks, instruction was turned over to several members of the staff.

Some of the more sensitive staff members recognized the need for flexibility and patience when dealing with Rod because of his bodily sabbatical. If his punches and kicks lacked finesse, or his rolls were angular or rocky, they cut him some slack, since he was doing well by just keeping up in the accelerated learning program. They knew things would smooth out over time, most likely a short time because of the rapid progress uchideshi training had provided students in the past.

There was one exception to the roster of staff members, an Instructor who didn't cut him any slack at all. He'd be teaching class, leading the warm-up and rolling exercises, then after spotting Rod doing something "incorrectly," the Instructor would single him out.

There's no doubt that individualized attention is great, but not when you stop the class to explain for all ears what this person is doing wrong, then add the additional pressure of performance anxiety on a beginning student, who's now forced to correct his mistake in front of everybody. Poor Rod was just trying to get through the class, and doing pretty well, all things considered. Living in the dojo, I'd seen a lot of beginners come and go, and seen much greater errors receive far less attention. Consequently, I couldn't believe he was isolating him like this.

Singling him out once or twice would have been helping him. Doing it every single class is humiliation under the guise of technical clarification. Clearly this was more for the benefit of the Instructor's ego, since he now had an excuse to exhibit for the class his vast wealth of knowledge.

If he had done this to me, it would have been OK. I can take it, but seeing it done to somebody else, especially my brother, was almost unbearable. I boiled. The Instructor had done a lot of egotistical things in the past, but I bit my tongue and rode them out. This, on the other hand, really tested me. I thought I was going to explode in every class he taught, but somehow managed to keep it under wraps.

His past behaviors should have clued me in to his teaching style.

During the warm-ups of a Saturday morning class he was leading, while most people are still in the process of waking up, the Instructor decided our rolls weren't quiet enough. Therefore, to really show us how tough his martial standards were, he took the class outside and had us do our entire ukemi sequence on a wooden deck.

Forward rolls, backward rolls, forward into backward rolls, forward sutemi (slapping with your hand at the bottom of a roll to absorb shock and shave speed), and backward sutemi were all dutifully executed. Luckily, the Instructor had enough sense to not have us do extended (jumping) rolls on the deck. It would have been certain death, especially with so many beginners in the class.

Aside from the bumps and bruises obviously incurred from this "exercise," more than one student bled from deck splinters (one of the black belts got one several inches long in his ankle), and our white gis were soiled with black residue from the wood. One student had just purchased a new gi and wore it for the first time that day. Worst timing ever.

Coming back inside the dojo, the Instructor continued to teach class. Having moved this black residue from the deck to our gis, we then transferred it from our gis to the white mat. Class ran overtime by twenty or thirty minutes as we scrubbed the mat on our hands and knees, trying to get it reasonably clean, as the Instructor supervised our efforts. Soon after, the Instructor took off, leaving behind the entire mess of buckets, mops, and towels.

And rightfully so. After all, that's the kind of training we were paying good money for: to pick up after other people's messes and tend to the wounds of their victims. Afterwards, the Instructor bragged about the whole thing. He seemed to think it was a good time.

Another incident involved a pretty girl who came to the dojo to observe a class. Shortly after she sat down, he set the class up with a technique from the kihon waza, and bowed off the mat to talk with her. Ten minutes went by, we were still doing the same goddamn technique, and the Instructor was long gone, captivated by his own conversation with this girl. After doing mae zemi dori thirty or forty times, students were conferring on changing techniques and whether or not the Instructor was ever coming back to us.

But he did. Twitterpated by the female presence, there had been a sudden change of plans. Sending us back to the side, he left no doubt that it was now "showtime." He demonstrated a few flashy techniques, which we worked on for a while, then in the last 10 minutes of class, he unveiled the finale.

He sat the class down and launched into a lecture on how ancient ninjas would dress as beggars and "accidentally" bump into samurai. Crunching vital areas while falling on their targets, the assassins would inflict lethal wounds before stumbling away, leading onlookers to believe the samurai had just taken a tumble and died. Then, ending the suspense, he demonstrated the technique a couple of times before ending class.

It was one of the worst things I'd ever sat through in my life. Aside from the fact that this was a jujutsu class and he was disseminating ninjitsu propaganda, all students had to bear witness to his attempt at impressing this girl.

Carolynn and I talked to her after class, and she ended up joining the dojo. Of course, the Instructor was all over her after that, soliciting her into private lessons, and hounding her with puppy dog devotion. Needless to say, she wasn't interested.

I was not alone in my observations or frustrations with the Instructor. Class after class, students would commiserate: "You know, after last time [the Instructor] taught, I didn't think things could get shittier. I was wrong." One visiting uchideshi was subjected to such condescension during a one-on-one session that he thought to himself, "That's it. I'm going to have to break this guy's arm. That's the only way he's going to respect me." He could have, too. That uchideshi had more belts, mat time, and fighting experience than the Instructor could imagine. I guess it's true whom God looks out for...

You might be wondering why Sensei was willing to put up with all this. First of all, from a physical standpoint, the Instructor was good. He put his time in on the mat and was a very solid, very technical practitioner. Second, it was his dream to be a martial arts instructor, and Sensei was working with him on achieving that goal. Third, most of his shenanigans were pulled while Sensei was out of town, so the only way Sensei would have known what was going on was feedback from students. But believe me, he got it.

I was getting ready for my shodan test at the time Rod came into the dojo. There was a lot of pressure in this, much of it self-induced. First of all, I wanted to do a fantastic job, something I would be proud of, something indicative of the years I had spent in martial arts and my dedication as an uchideshi. Next, being the first long-term resident uchideshi of the system and Sensei's pet project, I felt an outside expectation from those training at the dojo that this demonstration would be a very pure representation of what Seibukan Jujutsu was. The onus was on me to fully exemplify what this art was capable of at the shodan level.

Before any demonstration of a rank is performed, a pretest must be given by Sensei, a staff member, or senior yudansha (person with black belt rank). The pretest is really the test, allowing the student and teacher to fully pore over the requirements, without worrying about time restrictions, in a fairly relaxed atmosphere. The demonstration, what most people think of as the test, is really a public celebration of your skills as a martial artist. It is more rigidly structured, formalized, and intense from an emotional and physical perspective, because of the nerve-racking nature of public performance.

The pretest for my shodan exam was a little unusual. Instead of just picking a night and spending a few hours going straight through the requirements, Sensei broke the pretest up into small sections over three intermittent nights, using whoever happened to be loitering after class as uke. It was very informal, I passed everything, and the stage seemed set for a fun demonstration.

Sensei later informed me that there was some drama going on behind the scenes that I hadn't been aware of. Apparently, the Instructor had a problem with not being invited to the pretest. Never mind the fact that there was no official pretest done at a specified time, or that no one else had actually received a formal invitation. As he told Sensei in private meetings, he felt that he had given me more than anyone else, and basically, it was a slap in the face to not be invited.

In a way, I could understand his position, because he had helped me out by training with me when I first arrived at the dojo. But numerous people trained with me, offered instruction, and helped me out, so what was with the possessiveness? I think it was his ego acting out again.

You know, to be fair, the Instructor was not a "bad guy" or "evil person" if his ego wasn't called into play, but when it was ... man, you just couldn't believe it. Being "tough" with deck ukemi or showing off for a girl, those stories are just the tip of the iceberg, since an overblown ego has unlimited potential to make every situation agonizing. But I don't really think it was "him" as much as his ego. It had simply taken over.

But back to possessiveness. I could be wrong, but my impression was that in his mind, since he had helped me early on, that I was somehow "his," somehow obligated to become the Instructor's protégé, because of that early shot of instruction. But I wasn't his, I was Sensei's. I was his compatriot, not his student. I did come to Monterey to study under Sensei Toribio, and was living, eating, sleeping, and training in his dojo. I think that says something about where my loyalties were and should have been.

Of course the Instructor had a role in training me, but there were other staff members and training partners who had given me just as much, if not more, technical instruction. Sensei told him to talk to me about how he felt after my demonstration, not wanting to compound my stress level with yet another variable.

There's another thing about going for the level of shodan. Once you hit your ikkyu, the rank immediately before, it's customary to give something up, preferably something dear, as a sacrifice, a sign of renouncement. Some people give up drinking, smoking, coffee, or another vice of their choice. I chose to give up my hair. As my brother would attest, I was far too attached to grooming myself growing up. To fully realize the kind of asceticism I desired in this uchideshi experience, it was up to me to renounce my own vanity.

Besides, I had wanted to do it for the last couple of years, but never found a good opportunity to do so. Working for the government, winter in Alaska, trying to get a girlfriend, all of these were handy excuses for not taking my hair off. But now, living in a dojo, doing it as a symbol of devotion toward my goal, the timing was perfect. I had Sensei shave my head with some clippers at his house. Later that same night, I took off the final layer with a razor.

You might think, as I did, that having no hair would be a low-maintenance affair. You would be wrong. I went through a lot of razors and a lot of shaving cream trying to stay bald. Not having hot water at the dojo made things a little more difficult, but I managed to shave my scalp every other day. As a matter of fact, on the day of my shodan test, during my lunch break, I was in the middle of maintaining my asceticism when something unexpected occurred.

I heard someone open the front door of the dojo, and some undistinguished, yet vaguely familiar voices drifted back into the bathroom. I decided to check it out.

Try to imagine it: I'm walking across the mat, bare chested, one half of my head cleanly shaved while the other was covered in cream. Looking out on the visitors who had just walked in, I see my brother standing there with my mother and father, freshly flown in from Alaska.

Needless to say, this new image they saw didn't match their last recollection. Mildly shocked, they hugged me. They had to. It's a parent's job to be mildly shocked and love you anyway.

A few weeks earlier, Rod had seen another member of the dojo do his nidan (second degree black belt) demonstration, and my brother couldn't believe how many friends and family members came out of the woodwork to support the student. He realized that demonstrations for dan rankings were really a big deal, and promptly got in touch with our parents to see if they could make it down.

Obviously, they did, but to tell you the truth, I had mixed feelings about seeing them. Of course I loved my parents, and realized this was a rare opportunity to share a very meaningful aspect of my life with them, but having them there stressed me out, and I was already stressed enough. You understand, don't you? They're parents, that's what they do: they stress you out. That's part of their job, too.

Just lying in bed and visualizing different aspects of the demonstration got the butterflies going and my nervous system antsy. It was nothing more than a mental construct, but I knew that if I was getting this worked up just thinking about the demo, I was going to be in quite a state immediately beforehand.

I wanted to step up to the plate when all eyes were on me and expectations were high. I knew if I could suck it up despite all the distractions and stresses in this microcosmic demonstration, I'd be able to use this time as a touchstone for coming through moments of crisis for the rest of my life. This was going to be my personal rite of passage, and I wanted to be at my best.

I did the regular routine for a demonstration: buying flowers for the shomen (shrine), doing a thorough misogi (cleansing) of the dojo, then scrubbing and bleaching the mat. I participated in all the regular classes that Thursday, then, during the black belt class, my initiation into the Seibukan dan rankings began.

A formal Seibukan Jujutsu demonstration is one of the most powerful vehicles of self-expression I have ever seen, in or out of the realm of martial arts. It recreates all the pressure and anxiety of competition, without an external rivalry. You're facing yourself, and by putting yourself in the limelight, you're choosing to test and discover who you really are under duress. Those that are on the mat participating in the test, under Sensei's direction, will push you to your limits, but only in the spirit of support.

The first few demonstrations I witnessed blew me away in their emotional intensity and often left me in tears. I've always been a sucker for man at his best, and these demonstrations have often spurred individuals to break previously impenetrable barriers, and in a sense, forced people to extend beyond themselves, adding a new dimension to their identity.

Each demonstration begins the same. Sensei claps his hands twice, signaling that it's time to stop milling around and take their respective positions according to rank, in a formal line at the edge of the mat.

Sensei assumes his place at the head of the line, slightly offset, and barks, "Mokuso!" instantly quieting murmurs as students seated in seiza (kneeling position) engage in a silent meditation. After a minute or so, Sensei claps his hands, walks to the middle of the mat directly in line with the shomen, kneels, and leads us in bowing twice, clapping twice in unison, then bowing again. Sensei then turns to us and bows as we bow toward him, walks over to the side of the mat, and requests the assistance of the yudansha.

One by one, in quick succession, the yudansha stand and join Sensei at the side of the mat, leaving the testee alone. The demonstrator then knee-walks to the center of the mat, bows toward the shomen, turns, bows toward Sensei, turns, and bows to the yudansha on the mat. With a strong "Onegaishimasu (lit. I will be making a request)," the yudansha give their final blessing before the individual begins to demonstrate the physical requirements of that level.

The initiation has begun. At this point, the student is asked to start with ukemi, to illustrate his protective skills as a martial artist. Forward rolls, backward rolls, forward into backward rolls, sutemi, ushiro sutemi, extended rolls (jumping over three people), and ending with high falls from a variety of techniques Sensei chooses to throw you with. The first high fall is usually from an explosive kotegaeshi off a straight punch, then a nihonage shoulder throw from a side strike, followed by the ancient Daito-Ryu technique of yama-arashi (mountain storm), made famous by Shiro Saigo while defending the honor of the Kodokan.

After ukemi, the student and Sensei kneel, bow together, then kata is demonstrated. The kihon waza of the system, or 19 basic techniques, is the kata of the shodan level. While I was performing the techniques, only one thought went through my mind, "My God, he's going hard." The attacks were in such rapid succession, one quickly supplanted by another, that my mind shut off and my body automatically responded on its own. There was no time to ask what came next or to analyze the last technique. There was only that moment to respond with the appropriate answer to his attack, a physical payoff for the hours of kata practice on the mat.

Tai sabaki (body movement) is the next activity. Sensei will call up a yudansha he feels will serve as an appropriate uke, and commands him to attack. The attacks come in a pattern, so the student should be well prepared with an appropriate response. All too often, in the heat of the moment, memory fails and improvisation comes into play during sticky situations, which is fine.

Reversals, knife, gun, and jo (staff) defenses, a 12-bokken suburi, 40-movement jo kata, katana waza (sword hilt defenses) and katana goshinjutsu (sword takeaways), all of these areas must be executed effectively under the duress of the demonstration. Like all weapons in the shodan level, a set of basic attacks and defenses is learned, but during the demo, you don't know exactly how you're going to be attacked. Plus, they use show blades, which nudges the experience closer to an actual assault. The knife is real, but not terribly sharp, except near the tip. The katana is really an iaito, with an aluminum blade instead of steel. Again, it's not sharp along the edge (you can cut vegetables with them, but you'd really have to hack at an arm), but the tip is something to be wary of, since people have bled in demonstrations from both weapons.

Sensei is usually the one attacking with the sword, and when he gets that thing in his hand, watch out. Never trust him with a weapon, never turn your back, and always be on guard, since the energy he projects at this time is dark and serious. He wants you to realize that this is not a game, and feel the pressure of facing a person with malevolent intentions. Fortunately for us, his control is incredible, and he is able to push the student into matching his intensity. I've held my breath more than once while he attacked other students, and thought for sure one guy was going to lose his eye during his shodan demo with a sharp thrust from a pair of garden shears. Somehow though, under Sensei's direction, it remains safe.

The final taijutsu hurdle, henka, awaits the student after the aforementioned sections have been completed. Two yudansha are called up, one strikes, the other one grabs, and they attack the demonstrator, who's usually winded by now. After the student successfully defends himself he drops to his knees, two new attackers are chosen, and the demonstrator must execute techniques from that position, known as hantachi waza (half-standing techniques). After that's done, a chair is brought out onto the mat, two new attackers step up to the plate, and the student defends himself while seated. Finally, only one section remains to be completed to end a shodan demonstration: the secret weapon.

The secret weapon can be anything: a chain, hammer, butcher knife, whatever. Sensei is particularly fond of gardening implements, and has used a variety of them in the past. The rationale behind this section of the test is to instill in the student a lesson that no matter how well you may have prepared, you'll still have to deal with the unexpected. It's a carryover from his Ranger training, where the ability to improvise can mean the difference between life and death, for you and for others.

There was so much stress, expectation, drama, and exertion during my demonstration that it became a kind of transpersonal experience. Because I was on the spot, with only enough time to react to the attacks that were coming in, the "I" part of my psyche got lost since I didn't have the time for self-analysis, critique or congratulations. A shodan demonstration is continuous crisis management: a flurry of activity you cope with to the best of your ability. At the same time, if the observers know who you are, and are familiar with the art, they can see the clear connections between your personality characteristics and how they manifest as physical techniques.

It's all there, if you know what to look for, and it's fascinating how this kind of activity can put you in a space where you're not "thinking," which allows the real "you" to emerge.

I laid it all out on the line that night, and was satisfied with the effort. After I bowed out to the shomen, I kneeled before the line of yudansha and waited for each of them to say a few words and offer some feedback, as is customary. At the end of the line was my brother, the new uchideshi, kneeling in his yellow belt. Mudansha (non-black belt ranks) do not usually speak at the demonstrations, but because this was a special case, a special moment, Sensei allowed it. Rod bowed to me and tried to say something, but was overcome with emotion. Instead, he simply bowed again, which said it all. At that moment, there were few dry eyes in the room. Overall, it was a heavy experience, but a very good night.

A couple of days after my demonstration, I had a breakfast meeting with the Instructor, at a restaurant close to the dojo, in response to his invitation. We engaged in a little chitchat before he stated his position: He thought I was a good martial artist, and wanted to apologize for whatever he had done wrong. I accepted his apology but told him that there was nothing to apologize for. He went on to say that he must have done something wrong, even though he didn't know what it was, for me to not have invited him to my pretest.

I told him, quite frankly, that the thought of inviting him never came across my mind, just as I didn't invite anyone else. He contested this, counting out the number of days I was able to tell him that something was going to go on, and so forth.

No real progress was being made here, so after a while, I told him that one of the reasons we hadn't been getting along was the way he had treated my brother: repeatedly singling him out in class, demeaning him in an unforgettable fashion. The instructor contested this as well, stating that he was really only looking out for Rod's interests as an uchideshi, etc.

Eventually, I put it to him another way, although I really tried to phrase it as gently as I could. I told him that it could be construed that he was teaching classes out of ego, instead of the interests of the students, and he might want to take a look at that.

Instantly, I could see a steel wall drop, blocking out anything further I might say. Breakfast was over at that point, so we paid the bill. Before we went our separate ways, he offered me a ride to the dojo. I thanked him but told him I'd walk. It was only three blocks away.

Although the story of the Instructor ends there, Rod's saga went on. He continued to train after I left the dojo, and one year after he arrived in Monterey from Las Vegas, he tested for his shodan. Mom and Dad flew down from Alaska, and there was a big turnout that night to support him. It was a good test, but I was surprisingly unemotional through the whole thing. Maybe it's because, as an uchideshi, you're so over prepared for these things that I didn't fear for him. Later on it hit me, realizing what an accomplishment it was to have come from where he was, and achieve a goal that was neither easy nor certain. He even outdid me, living in the dojo 16 months, besting my own 15 month stay.

Even though he's not as addicted or obsessive as I am when it comes to martial arts, the year he spent as an uchideshi has given him a strong base of martial skills that will serve him for the rest of his life. But that's not the real gift Sensei gave him by offering the opportunity to come and live in Monterey.

The real gift granted was that now my brother and I can communicate in a different way, in another language. A language based on energy, motion, position, and timing. We have another common interest to increase our interactions, and another forum in which we can formulate goals and celebrate accomplishments.

Maybe this is what it's all about. Maybe martial arts are really about bringing people together, instead of learning how to fight. Maybe. I'm not sure if the aim of martial arts should be forming friends and linking families instead of learning techniques, but I can't deny it's a worthy goal. It brought my family together, if only for a while, and that's a technique I have yet to learn.

KI, CHRIS, AND KUNDALINI

One of the books that solidified my quest to become an uchideshi was Path Notes of an American Ninja Master by Glenn Morris.

When I first spied that Ken owned a copy, I didn't ask to borrow it, since I was sure it wouldn't have had anything of interest to me. After all, I wasn't a big ninjitsu fan.

But after seeing it lie there, week after week, in the dressing room of Aikido North, I read the back cover and was intrigued by the variety of topics, including seeing auras, kundalini, and meditation exercises toward enlightenment. I love enlightenment, so I devoured the book in a few sittings.

What really struck me was the way Morris described "enlightenment" as a concrete physiological process rather than a spiritual epiphany, being touched by God, or a cosmic paradigm shift. This gave me hope. I had assumed that enlightenment could only be achieved through long, arduous years in a Zen monastery, reflecting on koans (riddles) and thinking the elusive "thought which isn't a thought." Although enlightenment was penciled in as a lifetime goal, I didn't think I'd ever really enter a monastery and sit in front of a wall for eight hours a day. Eight hours is a long time.

Once, while in Japan, I was required to sit, relatively motionless, on a wooden floor while observing a ceremony. It probably wasn't more than three hours, but it will definitely be remembered as one of the most painful experiences in my life. My back had spasmed, my bottom was numb, and the mental anguish of knowing, "I'm not moving anytime soon," only magnified my level of discomfort. Although I'm sure the body would adapt and learn to relax in long meditation sessions, it still seemed to be a bit torturous, day in and day out. Overall, reaching for nirvana didn't seem like a good time.

But Morris' description of enlightenment put it back within reach. It was a refinement of the nervous system and rejuvenation of the hormonal system achieved through chi kung meditations. This provided the enlightened with lower respiration and heart rates, accelerated healing, unsuspected strength, increased fluidity of motion, greater pain tolerance, heightened sensitivity, enhanced creativity, and much, much more.

Who wouldn't want this? You may not be Superman, but you're certainly a step ahead of most mortal men with those additional tools at your disposal. I've always held out hope for a higher level in martial arts, one that transcends age, strength, and size. Morihei Ueshiba, the founder of aikido, certainly represents this kind of transcendence, as he was reportedly invincible from the time of his enlightenment until his death. Was this possible to attain? I hoped so, since it would certainly give me an edge in martial arts, not to mention in life itself.

Morris' own description of his expanded senses and capabilities wowed me, but he warned it wasn't easy, and he had paid some very heavy dues, including a marriage and a host of physical problems. In the end, though, it was worth it for him, and I knew that it would be worth it to me, regardless of the costs. I wanted that higher state of mind, and yearned to release the energetic potential lying dormant in my body.

All of this, of course, was taken on faith, as I had never had any firsthand experience with energetic phenomena. I had read an awful lot about it, but never really was able to experience something that I could put stock in, that I would swear was ki (vital energy), and not my imagination.

Long after I had read the book, and a few months before I actually left Alaska for Monterey, I had an interesting experience that tilted the scale of belief toward the existence of ki. I was training with Ken at Aikido North, and I persuaded him to do a quick adjustment on my back. Ken could crack my back better than anyone else I knew, and on that night, he followed it up with a little shiatsu. I sat on my knees, and following his directions, extended my arms out and breathed deeply as he probed my back. He noted that a particular point on my left side was "blocked", worked on it for a minute or two, then let me up. I felt the normal relief of a spinal adjustment, and went to the dressing room to change.

Ken and I sat there in the dressing room for a few minutes, chatting, when something very definite happened that I wasn't expecting. All of a sudden, I looked down at my hands and shouted, "What the hell?" as a wave of heat flooded them. I held them up, turned them over, and couldn't believe what I was feeling. My hands felt warm, instantly, with a pinprick sensation I can only approximate to falling asleep on your arm and letting the blood flow return. The "prickling," however, was more lightly distributed than a numb limb returning to life, and this heat rush lasted several minutes. Ken looked amused at my wide-eyed wonder and simply said, "You're welcome."

Finally, firsthand evidence that indicated to me that energetic phenomena were as real as Dr. Morris described them. It was a validation, a step in the right direction (I felt), and I wanted to share my experience with some of my friends who had similar interests. I eventually passed on my copy of <u>Path Notes</u> to my Brazilian Jiu-Jitsu training partners Eric and Chris.

Eric was already fairly well versed in the field of transpersonal psychology, with years of experience doing meditations and introspective analysis. Chris had little experience, but we had discussed the possibility of energetic phenomena and he seemed open minded. He even told me a story about a drummer he used to know who would sit in front of him and project "chi balls" a la Dragonball Z, so I figured it would be of interest to him as well.

I left my copy with them and headed to Monterey, hoping somehow that this uchideshi experience would assist me in the mind/body/spirit integration I had been striving for. I meditated occasionally at the dojo, but usually found myself too tired after training to augment it with anything, even sitting still.

I kept in touch with Eric, and tried to keep in touch with Chris, but he was a harder to track down. I spoke to him a few days after seeing the Ultimate Ultimate II on Pay Per View, and we had a great talk about how strong Ken Shamrock looked, the girl he was dating, what he was up to, etc.

One thing he mentioned that really stuck with me was his enjoyment of Path Notes, and the excitement of actual results gained from the meditations. He said, "I can really feel my chi moving around," and talked about how he could focus it into his hands. I thought that was great, he was certainly a lot further along than I was. We had a nice conversation, and it was good to get back in touch.

A few days later, I mentioned Chris' progress to Carolynn, and she was a little bit concerned about him focusing his energy into his hands. The monks at the Buddhist temple she attended had instructed her that moving energy around your body was OK as long as it was done in a circle, but keeping it in one place created an unhealthy energetic imbalance. I tried to contact Chris later and mention it, but couldn't get ahold of him.

All of this took place in the month of December, where my birthday seems to land, year after year. As a present to myself, I asked Sheila about embarking on some sort of shamanistic journey. I was pretty open to a variety of possibilities: hypnosis, past life regression, induced out-of-body experiences, vision quests, sweat lodges, whatever you call it, as long as it shifted my perspective, that's what I wanted. What I was looking for was a definite, real, and dramatic experience to expand my consciousness, under the safe supervision of an experienced guide. This kind of stuff is really popular in Northern California, so I was confident that

Sheila would be able to connect me with the proper people.

Sheila gave me a few names and numbers to call, but expressed regret that she didn't know about any Holotropic Breathwork sessions coming up in the near future. She thought it would be exactly what I was looking for.

"Holowhat?"

I had never heard of such a thing. My next question, of course, was asking if it was "real," in the sense that it produced a profound transformation in my thought processes, not easily written off as mere imagination. She promised me that her experience with it was very real, which Sensei confirmed, as he had participated in a session himself. I thought it was unfortunate that they didn't know where I could contact people doing that kind of work, but dialed the other numbers Sheila had given me and tried to organize my "trip."

A few weeks later, a flyer came to the dojo through the mail, billed as "The Adventure of Self-Discovery." It was, wouldn't you know it, a notification of a Holotropic Breathwork seminar conducted by the man himself, Stanislav Grof.

Stanislav Grof, M.D., is a former professor at Johns Hopkins University School of Medicine and former Chief of Psychiatric Research at the Maryland Psychiatric Research Center. While enrolled in medical school in Prague, he volunteered to be an experimental subject for the drug LSD-25. Profoundly moved by the experience, he later conducted LSD research, convinced of the enormous healing potential of non-ordinary states of consciousness, especially over traditional methods such as psychoanalysis, which had shown poor clinical results. Later, he developed a drug-free method of inducing non-ordinary states of consciousness known as Holotropic Breathwork, using evocative music, altered breathing patterns, and bodywork. Grof is considered one of the most brilliant minds in psychology today, and I was excited at this opportunity to engage in a clinically verified and scientifically directed spiritual awakening.

Carolynn was just as intrigued as I was by the seminar, and promptly bought his book "The Holotropic Mind" to better understand the philosophy behind the breathwork technique we'd be employing. After she was finished, she loaned it to me, expecting me to read it. I actually expected to read it as well, but never got around to it.

Carolynn and I drove through a torrential rainstorm to San Raphael in late January to take part in the seminar. It was held in a hotel designed for modestly sized conventions, and we checked in on Friday afternoon, early enough to rest up before Stan's evening lecture.

Smart move. To hear such a learned man succinctly explain and clearly describe the often inaccessible subject of non-ordinary states of consciousness was impressive by itself, even more so since English is his third language. We had a giant in our midst, and the audience at large appreciated and revered his insight and experience.

After the lecture, the room was divided into several groups, each one circled in a different area of the room, composed of 20 to 25 members. All introduced themselves and explained why they were participating in the course. Each group also had a few facilitators experienced with the Holotropic Breathwork method, ready to answer questions or provide assistance when necessary. One of the more effeminate male facilitators extended an open invitation to "come by room 206 if you have any other questions ... or just need to talk." Hmmm... thanks anyway.

Carolynn and I retired fairly early, waking up the next morning in time for a leisurely breakfast, provided by the hotel. The day was split into two breathwork sessions, one in the morning, one in the afternoon. Carolynn decided she would go first, as the breather, while I would act as the sitter, attentive to and responsible for her needs. That was fine with me, since unleashing my subconscious this early in the morning usually resulted in a mix of profanity and profound negativity.

We had been instructed to bring whatever we felt would be necessary to make our session more comfortable. Some brought sleeping bags and pillows, but Carolynn and I just borrowed some sofa cushions and blankets from the hotel room and laid them down, claiming space in the crowded convention room. We were definitely not alone. At least a hundred other participants were present, half of them preparing their beds for their imminent departure, the other half standing by as the breathers' babysitters. Finally, the time had come.

Over the cushions and under the blankets, Carolynn lay down and tried to relax. The lights were deeply dimmed, Stan gave some final remarks before bidding us to "have a nice trip," then turned the music up. The Scandinavian group Hedningarna blasted from the speakers, and across the floor, chests heaving heavily, in and out, up and down.

I had expected that the breathing cadence required to achieve an altered state of consciousness would be far more complex, similar to kundalini yoga or other tantric traditions. You know, timed inhalations, drawing breath through a specific nostril, holding it for certain counts, etc. None of that was necessary. Stan simply told us to breathe a little more deeply and a little more rapidly than usual, and continue for the desired duration of the experience. This, coupled with foreign music, is what launched the breather into psychedelic nether, since the mind is never given the opportunity to latch on to an English word and the breathing is paced to the music's beat.

As I looked around the room, bellies heaving with audible exhalations, I thought that it would probably be awhile before people started to feel the effects of the breathing technique. I couldn't have been more wrong. In under 40 seconds, people moaned and their bodies began twitching. In less than five minutes, men and women were screaming at the top of their lungs while facilitators restrained those who were thrashing or partially convulsing.

I couldn't believe it. Initially, I thought to myself, 'No way. These people have got to be faking it,' but it didn't matter if they were or not: they weren't stopping and certainly weren't shutting up. You'd think people were being butchered with machetes by the intensity of their screams. Social conventions held no sway on this group.

Bodies writhing in agony or ecstasy, strewn crazily around a crowded room, with attendants hovering over them; the whole scene was reminiscent of nurses trying to ease the pain of fallen soldiers after battle. I must admit, it was disturbing, and I could completely understand why Carolynn had a difficult time feeling safe enough to really let go and push the experience to its potential. How could you when you're stuck in a room full of random people, psychic energy bouncing off the walls, while their current problems and past life baggage is immediately brought to the forefront of their consciousness?

In short, Carolynn was frustrated with the experience and I don't blame her. She felt a tremendous, overwhelming sense of sorrow during the two and a half hour session, largely due, I feel, to the setting.

Who wants to pay $225 for an experience so depressing that it lingers for days? Not me. I can feel that way in the privacy of my own home for far, far less.

After a light lunch, it was my turn, and I didn't know what to expect. I had tried to achieve out-of-body experiences in the past, but never got very far. I was looking forward to exploring alternate dimensions, but no matter how many books I read or exercises I tried, I couldn't separate an inch from my body. I was a transpersonal failure and I knew it. I secretly wondered if I'd get anything out of this seminar at all, seeing how my former expectations and desires probably hindered past progress. I hoped for the best, but what else could I do?

I lay down on the cushions, under the blankets, with a towel over my eyes to block extraneous light. Carolynn was right at my side as the music began. In, out, in, out, my lungs forcefully expanded and contracted at a constant rate, slightly faster and deeper than normal respiration. Less than a minute into it, much to my chagrin, I felt something in the palm of my right hand.

It was a tingling sensation, but one more akin to an electric current than a pinprick. I continued breathing, and the energy engulfed my forearm and hand. This was unbelievable, and I thought to myself, "Yes, this is it!" I barked orders to Carolynn to grab my hand and feel how hot it was. She complied, but contrary to my expectation, she reported that my hand felt clammy. Strange, it felt tangibly hot to me.

Beginning in the palm of my hand, the energy continued up my limb, worked its way across my chest, and dropped down the left arm. Over the next hour and a half, it slowly spread from my torso down my hips, to my legs, all the way to my toes. Every part of my body that conducted this energetic phenomenon felt exceedingly warm, and I swore every cell in those areas was vibrating robustly, like magnified Brownian motion.

Based on previous readings, I thought I would have felt the energy surge from the base of my spine through the chakras. Honestly, I didn't feel any energy, in any way, emanating directly from that point, but don't mistake that for disappointment. What I was feeling was as real as any armbar or choke I've ever tapped to. My imagination wasn't involved in the slightest; this was purely physical.

My body-at-large was brimming with a force I couldn't fully control, and from the beginning I had assumed the position of a crucified man. My arms were held out at my sides, not as a voluntary decision or a Catholic tribute, but out of physical necessity. I felt best in this position, because my mobility was so stifled by this energy coursing through my body.

Now, if I concentrated my attention and really tried, I could move. But this took considerable effort on my part, and besides, there was no reason to. I was savoring every moment of this experience, as I knew it might never happen again.

I've tried to find a good analogy to convey what I was feeling, and the best one I can refer to is the guideline used by aikidoka for the "unbendable arm" exercise:

Imagine your arm is like a firehose, with torrents of water flowing through it toward a distant point. The hose can't bend until the internal pressure drops, just as I found it difficult to bend my arms as my extension was energetically supported from the inside out. That really is the most accurate description of what I felt.

I should mention that the experience was not entirely painless. Early on in the session, as the energy surged down my left arm, I felt a searing pain in my left wrist. Months earlier, I suffered an injury from a lightning fast kotegaeshi, and my tendons were still recovering. I don't know if my damaged paw was an energetic obstacle that needed to be burned through, or the energy was working to heal it, but I know that it hurt, and I had to ask Carolynn to fetch a facilitator to work on it for a while. They massaged it and it definitely felt better, but still wasn't good as new.

As the session wore on, through a combination of visualization and willpower, I tried to move this energy up my body, up my spine, and shoot it through the top of my head. My thinking was, "Well, since I'm having a kundalini experience, I might as well go for the big time."

But I couldn't do it. The best that I could do was make my neck and jowls tingle, and that's where it stopped. Shortly thereafter, the friendly facilitator from room 206 laid down next to me, propped his head on his hand, and instructed me to begin slowing down, since the session would be finishing soon. I did as he asked, and returned to breathing normally, as I felt this internal, vibratory power recede to an imperceptible level.

The facilitator stopped me way too early, I realize now that I look back on it, as others continued to scream for at least another half an hour. I think he just wanted to chat, since he continued to loiter next to me in my fragile condition. Carolynn didn't like him hanging around, and she was in a far better position than I to see things as they really were.

My body settled, I removed the towel from over my eyes, opened them, and saw Carolynn's face hovering above me. I had never been more thankful to see anyone in my life, and an overwhelming sense of safety, peace, and acceptance flooded through me. It was incredible. I want to feel that way every time I wake up. I laid there for a few more minutes, and when I thought I was ready, I bent at my waist and tried to sit up.

Bad move. I fell back down instantly, with little muscular resistance slowing me. I was surprised at my own lack of strength and balance, so I waited a bit longer, maybe five minutes, and tried it again. This time, I succeeded at sitting up, and paused for a moment at the top, steeling myself for the next risky maneuver. When I felt I was ready, I spun out on to my knees and tried to stand. Instead, I fell down face first back into the sofa cushions. I continued to lie there, celebrating my decision to rest a bit longer.

Eventually I got up and we left the room, heading for our next activity: drawing mandalas. I wasn't really into it, nor was I into showing those mandalas before we shared our experiences in a debriefing session with our original group members. The meeting was well intentioned, though, and it was interesting to hear the vast array of experiences possible with the Holotropic Breathwork method.

Two other people in our group also had energetic phenomena surface in their bodies, so I realized my experience wasn't that unusual. Overall, I was pleased with my session, having felt some sort of confirmation had taken place that my mystical aspirations were achievable, and I wasn't the transpersonal failure I once thought I was. Part of me thinks one reason I may have been successful was that I did have relatively low expectations, with only the most basic familiarity with the method. I'll have to remember that next time: Don't read the book.

On the other hand, a number of people had delved into unpleasant realms of their psyche, and were uncertain if this was good for them at all. One woman met up with her long dead, heavily despised mother-in-law, and feared going back home to her husband since she knew that his mother's spirit was hanging around, watching them, and rooting for disaster.

Another man, an experienced Breathwork veteran, choked back the tears long enough to tell us of his abduction by aliens, that this was by far the worst experience of his life, and his vow to never do anything like it again. And to think this poor bastard paid $225. He should have come over to my place.

Carolynn and I returned to Monterey, and I shared my story with a few friends that I knew would appreciate it. Sheila and her mother Martha, also an energy worker, both thought it fortunate that I wasn't successful in shooting the energy through my skull. They explained why, and although I was already familiar with the lore, I absorbed a few more horror stories of a premature kundalini awakening and its resulting problems, ranging from long-term insomnia to hallucinogenic psychosis.

I called Eric in Alaska to share my experience, since he was already familiar with the subject, and just as I thought, he found it just as interesting as I would have had he called me to relay the story. We kept in touch over the year, and he kept me up to date with Chris, whom I could never manage to contact directly.

Over a period of months, as Eric gave me pieces of information, the following scenario took form: Chris was having difficulty holding down a job, so Eric gave him one at his embroidery shop. Everything went well at first, but within a few weeks a change occurred in Chris, which Eric relayed to me as: "It was almost as if his personality fragmented," and "He couldn't hold his attention on anything for more than two minutes a time." Eric even described him babbling, almost uncontrollably, and when he inquired what the problem was, Chris replied with equal concern, "I don't know. I . . . I can't help it."

Things weren't working out at the shop, so regrettably, Eric let Chris go, and he made his way back to live with his mother in Virginia, hoping to do better there.

Before I left Alaska, I made Chris promise to look out for a girlfriend of mine named Melissa. Ironically, it was Melissa who kept me informed on what was happening with Chris, as he returned to Alaska to sling bags one more summer at my favorite job. She told me he just didn't look the same and generally seemed pretty down. She said he brightened when she suggested he give me a call, but he never did. Elusive again, I assumed he returned to Virginia after the summer.

The next word I received about Chris was several months later, after I had moved out of the dojo. I was relaxing at home with my roommates when the phone rang. I picked it up, and realized it was Eric calling from Alaska. I was happy to hear from him and in good spirits when he gravely asked, "Did you hear?"

"Hear about what?" I responded.

"Oh, I guess not." He paused. "It's about Chris."

"What about him?" I asked, but it had already hit me. I already knew.

"He's dead."

On January 23, 1998, Chris died at 22 years of age. No cause of death is listed on the obituary; it simply states he died in his home.

I don't think the meditations he engaged in hurt him in any way, but coupled with other factors in his life, I don't feel they helped him at the stage where he was at. Chris liked to party, he had a stressful relationship with his girlfriend, financial strains to remain independent, plus the additional challenges life threw at him as a young male establishing his identity in this society.

I don't know what to think, and I don't know what to say, but some things pop up unconsciously. Bright. Charismatic. Witty. Refined. Those are the words that come to mind when I think of him. Chris had an insight and appreciation for life that struck something in me, and with that, established an immediate bond between us. It's rare, but when it does happen, I look at those people as kindred spirits. There aren't that many that come your way. Once you've made that contact, you realize what you have and hate to see them go.

I think of the last time I saw him, dropping him off at his house after a sparring session. I was leaving the next day, and we both expressed remorse that circumstance had only allowed us to hang out for such a short time. We shook hands, shared a goodbye, and climbing out of the car, Chris got ready to close the door.

But instead of shutting it, he leaned across the seats, stuck his hand out again, and said, "Hey... one more good-bye."

Maybe I'll see him the next time around, and the moment we cross paths again, that bond will reconnect despite lifetimes of distance. In that moment, we may realize that no time has passed at all. I look forward to that day, Chris, and hope to see you soon.

SOMEONE WATCHING OVER

It was another crowded Thursday night class, Sensei was teaching, and he showed a technique I had seen only once before in my life. It really surprised me.

Because I had been studying both Brazilian Jiu Jitsu and Seibukan at the same time, knowledge was being amassed at both ends, and I'd often try to combine elements from each to find new techniques, or at least different ways of getting into them. Such was the case here.

It was an armbar formed by triangling the legs, something I had never seen before, something that had just come to me in a dream the night before.

So there it was, the triangled leg armbar I had never seen in real life, demonstrated for the class. Now it was our turn. I grabbed a good friend as a training partner, and tried it out. We did it a few times, and since I knew him, I decided to share my little precognitive shocker. By his lack of response, I assumed he was unimpressed, and we continued to train in a lighthearted manner.

At work the next day, that friend called me up and asked if I had a minute, since he had something to tell me. He also mentioned that he'd appreciate it if I didn't speak about this to anyone else, since they might not react to it favorably.

You see, he had a long history of psychic occurrences stemming back to childhood, but rarely mentioned them to anyone other than close friends for fear it would affect his business.

"Hey Roy, do you remember when we were in the room at the back of the house?" He was referring to a small office that had been built behind his main house, where we had been chatting through the evening, about nothing in particular.

"Yeah, of course."

"Well," he continued, "since you had mentioned you had dreamt that technique Sensei was showing, I kind of took that as a sign that I should share this with you. I wasn't going to mention it before, but I think you should know. There was somebody in the room with us that night."

"Are you serious? What do you mean?"

"I'm totally serious. Just to the left of you, when you were sitting in that chair, I saw a woman staring right at me. It wasn't all of her, it was just the top portion... you know, just the chest and head.'"

I was flabbergasted. This was not a man who would make something like this up, have anything to gain by telling me, or ingest hallucinogenic substances. He was a straight-arrow, professional family man, describing something he felt was very real, and taking a chance by sharing information that others would ridicule.

I had to know more. "So you could really see her, clearly, and she was real, I mean, she wasn't just...?"

"I could see her just as clearly as I could see you," he assured me. Then he went on to describe her. She was a small woman, about five feet four, 70 to 75 years old, with strong Mexican or Italian features, and old-age spots on her skin. She had long, straight, coarse hair, black giving way to gray, and she was emanating a message to my friend. Unmistakably, it came through to him as this: "We are watching over."

Is there someone watching over? I hope so. Sometimes I need somebody to keep me from going over the line: serving martial arts instead of having them serve me.

Originally, I set out to invest myself fully in martial arts as simply a means to an end: achieving a higher state of consciousness and reaping physical benefits along the way. But more and more often, as I trek down this path, I find myself distracted by delving into deeper realms, and paying heavy tolls for the distances I've traveled.

At times my training has eclipsed more pressing priorities, which begs the question "Who is serving whom?" Whether it's born from insecurity or compulsion, this urge to train has to have some sort of check to achieve a sense of balance. For me, I'm discovering that my body is the ultimate limiting factor. I pop and crack a lot for someone who's 24. At some point, I'm going to have to take a long break. Maybe that's part of the discipline, too.

People who knew me supported my ambition because they realized my passion, even if they secretly feared for me. My boss at the NTSB gave his own brand of tacit approval by barking commands at me in the office: "Royboy...CREAN DOJO! My parents supported my goals, even if they didn't fully understand them, and my family of training partners at Aikido North encouraged me to take a chance. But support was not universal.

When I explained to acquaintances, or to my friends' parents, my plan to live as an uchideshi, the first question I always received was, "Oh, and what are you going to do with that?" Then, after the inquisition, came the mourning. "God, and what about your music? You're giving it up for that?" I understood their lament, but doesn't sacrificing something dear to you make martial arts mean that much more? I think so.

I started out with a pretty mystical take on martial arts, but ended up as a pragmatist. The underlying secret of martial arts I wanted to know is the one I knew all along. It's training. Mat time. All things come through this.

Ki, energy extension, whatever you want to call it, does exist, and plays a part in technique, but as far as I can tell, it's icing on the cake. Maybe ki is like talent. It's present in everyone, some people have more of it than others, and you really can cultivate it, but don't ever, ever rely on it. Let me repeat that: don't ever rely on it. If you do, you'll pay a price you never could afford.

Is there someone watching over? I'd like to think that there is. I feel that I took a blind leap of faith, pursuing some archaic ideal as an adventure, stepping out into the unknown on an uncleared path. Miraculously, I came to the right place, under the right instructor, who had more than just a school and a need for another body willing to undergo hard training. It wasn't merely Sensei's technical knowledge, ranks, physical prowess, or students that made this the right place. All of that played a part, of course, but there's more.

It was his honesty, openness, and willingness to experiment. I mean, how many instructors would have let me study under another teacher while I was living in their dojo? Not many, but every time he let me go, he won me back again.

The most important thing though, all things considered, was his positive intention. He gave me an opportunity to have the uchideshi experience he wished he'd had, in a system he designed and would have liked to have studied at my age. He genuinely wanted me to get the most out of my year, his heart was in it, and that made the difference. Technique without heart is hollow, and so is instruction.

What I've written is a collection of experiences, incomplete in its reenactments even as a finished work. It's difficult to remember a year in its entirety, and there was more that happened in my time as an uchideshi than I covered in these pages: I walked on fire, saw U2 in concert, and flew to Ft. Lauderdale during spring break, only to see the cruise ship I intended to board pull away from the dock, overbooked with passengers.

There were disappointments, but these were offset by physical progress and the achievement of my goals: I was training, I was learning, and I was getting better.

But every so often, in the thick of this physical training, something very subtle would occur. Unintentionally, I would stumble into what I've called an open moment. It's difficult to describe, but in the middle of whatever I was doing, something came over me that made me think, "This is it."

There's wasn't any reason to look beyond where I was. My mind wasn't jumping ahead to the next step. I was just half a beat ahead of the cadence and suddenly fell into sync as the moment began to expand. It's a fleeting state of mind, but things like that remind me that the discipline of martial arts has a lot going on beneath the surface of fighting techniques.

Is there someone watching over? I hope so. After all, we're just a minute of hypoxia from screaming and chaos. Without some sort of guidance from above, I wonder if people would be able to find the right teacher who can give them what they need. Perhaps, but it's a big world, which leaves a lot of space to miss making connections. As for my experience, although it would be impossible to prove, I'm starting to suspect that someone may have had a hand in it. Of course I'll never know, but it all worked out.

Maybe that's proof enough.

THE JOURNEY CONTINUES

The next step in the journey was to move south and continue my education, on the mat, and at university.

I had no idea the lessons I would learn.

I had been accepted into another kind of learning program at the University of California, San Diego, in a progressive media technology course. SoCal beckoned me.

After 3 years of living in Monterey, I completed my martial apprenticeship with Sensei Toribio with a shodan demonstration in aikido, and a sandan demonstration in Seibukan Jujutsu. I can't thank him enough for his guidance, wisdom and support. He is truly a master.

Southern California was a new beginning and a chance to focus on emerging technologies, both martial and musical. I met another great teacher who would change me forever, Professor Roy Harris. Under him I furthered my understanding of Brazilian Jiu Jitsu, leading me to the rank of black belt and beyond.

Just as I've shared my adventures in judo, aikido, and Japanese jujutsu in this book, I am excited to bring readers through my BJJ Journey in the next.

It has been the most amazing adventure...

ABOUT THE AUTHOR

Roy Dean is a leader in martial arts, media, and the use of jiu jitsu as a vehicle for self development.

Professor Dean holds third degree black belts in Seibukan Jujutsu and Brazilian Jiu Jitsu, with additional black belts in Judo and Aikido.

You can follow his latest explorations at roydean.tv.

Copyright © 2016 by Roy Dean

Names and identifying details of some of the people and places in this book have been changed.

All rights reserved.

You connect with us here:

contact@roydean.tv

Photos by Rick Ellis

Printed in Great Britain
by Amazon